Original publication: "Hudební nauka Klíček 4"
Author: Eva Šašinková, M.M., Ph.D., M.B.A.
Illustrations: Mgr. Kateřina Kovářová
Original graphic design: Lumír Kaděra
Original publisher: Czech Music Edition, Prague, Czech Republic, 2022
Website: www.hudebni-publikace.cz
Copyright: Eva Šašinková, M.M., Ph.D., M.B.A.
Original Czech version ISBN: 978-80-907578-7-5

English adaptation: "Clefi's Music Notebook 4"
Illustrations: Mgr. Kateřina Kovářová
Translation, adaptation, and graphic design: Roman Placzek, D.M.A.
Publisher: BumbleBee Notes™ Music Publishing, Manlius, NY, USA, 2025
Catalog number: cbbn002-wb-009
Website: www.bumblebeenotes.com
Copyright: BumbleBee Notes™ Inc. Music Corporation
ISBN: 979-8-9919035-8-5

Clefi's Little Crossword Review

Down:
1. A high female voice.
2. A lowered derived interval.
3. The enharmonically exchanged note D flat.
4. A fifth chord built on the fourth degree.
6. The major scale fundamental interval.
8. A fifth chord built on the first degree.
10. dim3.
15. The C major subdominant.
17. The minor scale with one sharp.
19. A C clef (violas).
21. A C clef (cellos).
22. A raised derived interval.

Across:
5. The lowest vocal.
7. A small instrumental ensemble.
9. 9/8 meter.
11. The primary tone row.
12. The first inversion of a fifth chord.
13. A fifth chord built on the fifth degree.
14. The enharmonically exchanged G flat major scale.
16. A complete notation of a musical composition.
18. A measure with just one heavy beat.
20. Two four-tone sections of a diatonic scale.
23. The minor scale fundamental tone.
24. The minor scale with two flats.

Eva Šašinková, M.M., Ph.D., MBA, the author of the series, lives in Prague, Czech Republic, where she concertizes and holds academic positions at the Pilsen Conservatory and Academy of Music in Prague. Since childhood, Eva has dreamed of becoming a music teacher, sharing her passion and experience of love for music, especially with children. She has a deep love for the double bass, her instrument, in which she holds a master's degree. However, Eva also profoundly admires the piano, an instrument that was an inseparable part of her

About the Author

childhood. This admiration is the reason behind the concept of her method, which she based on the keyboard's layout. Eva is convinced that the piano is a unique instrument designed to help explain the fundamentals of music theory, the meaning of tones and melody, and the mission of music. She successfully proves her firm conviction in the practical application of her method. The story of her project started with a children's story that came to life during a trying period in the author's life.

Her passion for teaching children and desire to share her knowledge helped her concentrate on the essentials. During her pedagogical activities, Eva noticed that the materials available to her for the curriculum presentation were not, in her professional opinion, satisfactory. She started to visit music schools in her home country, the Czech Republic, comparing, editing, reworking, and creating. As a result, Eva began to bring worksheets filled with information and fun activities to the music education classes to make students' time learning music theory more engaging, easily accessible, and entertaining. The reactions of the young music students and fellow pedagogues were overwhelmingly positive.

Professor Eva managed to engage children's senses from all angles—drawing, singing, and practical demonstrations on a keyboard—everything children appreciated. On top of that, she had "The Story of a Song, "which kicked off a star career for one little boy, Clefi. He welcomes children in his "Clefi's Little Notebook" and helps them learn more in the four volumes of his "Clefi's Music Notebook." He plays and sings with them in "Clefi's Little Music Education Notebook" (in the translated version integrated into "Clefi's Little Notebook" – editor's note) and "Clefi's Musical Instruments" written for little musicians. Clefi helps them practice their newly acquired knowledge in three workbooks full of fun tasks and exercises. Children play with little Clefi, learn, and get ready for the more dedicated encounter with Lady Music and their chosen instrument in a fun and engaging way. And maybe it will become the love of their lives, their calling, and a hobby, as it happened to the author.

And to the sad faces of those who did not have the luck to learn from the best teachers and publications and did not have the best opportunities, Eva says with her clever little smile: "If you love music and have an open heart, the muse will not ask you how old you are. She will kiss you on the brow when you least expect it. So do not wait and be ready!"

Author's Foreword

Clefi's New Music Education School

is a unified music education method for children, amateur musicians, and music students.

Based on my extensive multi-genre musical performing career, many years of experience teaching children, and my terminal education degree in music theory, I have created a unified music education program for children from an early age to young musicians who choose to study music more seriously. The New Music Education School leans on children's natural perception of music. It offers young musicians and their teachers a unified educational system of fundamental music theory aiming to support musical creativity. Its main goal is to awaken children's musicianship based on creativity and the ability to sing a song, play it on a musical instrument of their choice, and write it down correctly, the sort of musicianship that enables them to use their musical knowledge theoretically and practically.

The first book, Clefi's Little Notebook, is tailored for the youngest musicians. It introduces us to Clefi, a charming little boy who shares his story. Clefi becomes our companion on this musical adventure. In Clefi's Little Notebook, children delve into musical notation, the birth of a song, a musical note, a musical staff, a clef (which inspired Clefi's name), the musical alphabet, and a scale. They learn to read and write notes in the fourth, the middle octave, and practice their new skills through exercises, puzzles, engaging tasks, and songs they play and sing.

Clefi's Music Notebooks 1, 2, 3, and **4** follow Clefi's Little Notebook. These four full-color music textbooks stand out for their unique conceptual design. Each volume is a complete unit and can be used individually.

At the same time, all four volumes are designed as one method, seamlessly following one another, so that the children can acquire a complete knowledge of the fundamentals of music theory in a friendly and engaging way.

Beautiful illustrations and graphic design enhance the unique quality of these lovely publications. All textbooks are suitable for children, amateur musicians, and professional music students.

This music education series explains the fundamentals of music theory quickly and efficiently so that children can understand and practice them while playing musical instruments, singing, and harmonizing. The textbooks aim to develop children's musical abilities, aural skills, perception of tone pitch and duration, and rhythmical and tonal melodic structure.

The idea behind this methodological concept is to make children first listen, then understand, learn, utilize, and create. When born, a baby listens and absorbs speech. When it understands it, it tries to pronounce the first words. A child attempts to understand the connections and context. Only after several years can a child logically think and systematically create. And the same applies to the understanding of music! What would the knowledge of music theory be for if we did not listen to music and didn't use the ingenious system of music theory in practice? However, the same applies both ways. How can we expect to evolve in our music-making if we refuse to learn and explore the mysteries of music, its tonal relations, harmony, and rhythm?

This method will help children fully absorb music and learn essential human and life values through it. We can learn to read and write only if we listen to our parents talk from an early age. Then, we learn the words, pronounce them, and understand their meaning. The same applies to music and how we understand it.

I hope my books will bring you joy and help many young musicians open the door to the beautiful world of music.

Eva

What's Inside:

Clefi's Little Crossword Review i
About the Author ii
Author's Foreword iii
What's Inside iv
Clefi's Greeting v
Pitch Class System 1
Musical Notation 2
Rhythm, Measure 4
Accidentals, Enharmonic Tones 6
Intervals 7
Types of Scales 10
Diatonic Scales 11
Modern Major & Minor Scales 12
Old Church Scales 14
"Parsley, Sage, Mint, Bit of Basil" 16
"Wars Have Happened This Year" 16
"A Little Cuckoo Bird is Calling" 17
"When I Was at My Mom's Place" 17
Chromatic & Whole-Tone Scales 18
Exotic Scales 19
Key, Chord 20
Types od Chords 21
Major & Minor Fifth Chord 22
Diminished & Augmented Fifth Chord 23

Seventh & Ninth Chord 24
Basic Types of Chords Overview 25
Chord Symbols 26
Commonly Used Chords 27
Chord Inversions 28
Chord Inversion Chord Symbols 29
Exercises 30
Fundamentals of Harmony 32
Melody Harmonization 36
Musical Terms in Harmony 38
Exercises 39
Music Terminology 40
Tempo 41
Articulation 42
Musical Expression, Performance
Techniques 43
Dynamics 44
Melodic Ornamentation 45
Repetition Signs & Markings 46
Grand Review 47
Professional Music Disciplines 50
CERTIFICATE OF COMPLETION vi
Answer Key to Clefi's Little Crossword
Review vii

Similar to "Clefi's Little Notebook," this book presents a collection of enchanting folk songs from the rich Czech folklore tradition, designed for music education. To accurately utilize their intended purpose, each song requires accurate adaptation and translation into English, which would take up more space than these volumes can accommodate without disrupting their intended design. Therefore, we are offering a standalone "Clefi & Notelina's Songbook," featuring all the songs from all nine volumes of Clefi's New Music Education School series, along with accurately and sensibly translated and adapted English lyrics.

Dear musical friends,

As we approach the final round of our journey, we invite you to join us on an inspiring adventure around the world.

Together, we have gathered the essential knowledge to further master our musical artistry. Our strong foundation in music theory sets the stage for us to construct music structures of limitless creativity. In this final Clefi's Music Notebook, we will review and practice everything we've learned. We'll also explore the world of accomplished musicians and music professionals.

We will start with the basics of conducting. The Leaning Tower of Pisa will remind us how to manipulate tones and use enharmonic exchanges. Then, the Statue of Liberty will guide us through musical intervals.

As we travel the world, we will examine various scales across different cultures and historical periods. For the first time, we will study the old church scales that helped form the modern major and minor scales. We will also discover scales consisting only of whole or half steps and learn how some Asian countries use the Pentatonic scale.

At the pyramids, we will learn about chord structures and symbols. Once we understand how to create seventh and ninth chords, we will climb the Eiffel Tower. From the top, we will see that the basics we learned may seem simple, but they are essential for building larger musical structures. After this climb, we will have a clear way to explore chord symbols.

The next stage of our journey will involve a cruise on a large ocean liner to the Harmony Archipelago, where a musical path awaits us. However, that's not all; after our visit, we will need to find our way home. We will be guided by signs featuring musical terminology, articulation, and dynamic markings that lead us to the station, where an express train is waiting. This train will be driven by someone who ensures the correct tempo is maintained. Do you know his name? If not, you'll have to wait to find out!

Will you stay with us until the final plane takes flight, unveiling the endless musical horizons we have yet to explore? If you do, we congratulate you on your incredible journey filled with musical wonders and wish you continued success in your musical artistry.

May the doors to the enchanting world of music always be wide open for you, filling your life with boundless joy and inspiration that never fades!

Yours,
Clefi and Notelina

PITCH CLASS SYSTEM

Tones are sounds characterized by a consistent rate of vibrations or a regular frequency. They have precise pitches and can be sung or played on musical instruments. In contrast, all other sounds are classified as noises. **Noises** arise from irregular vibrations in various forms of matter - such as the roar of an engine, the crashing of ocean waves, or the howling of the wind.

The fundamental characteristics of tones are duration, pitch, volume, and color.
Tone Duration: Tones can be either long or short.
Tone Pitch: Tones can range from high to low or fall somewhere in between.
Tone Volume: Tones can be loud or extremely soft.
Tone Color: Human voices and various musical instruments produce tones with distinct characters, known as tone color.

PITCH CLASS SYSTEM

The pitch class system organizes all tones according to their pitch. At its core are **seven primary tones**, known as the primary tone row: **C-D-E-F-G-A-B**. These tones repeat at various pitch registers. Arranging the tone rows across different registers helps maintain clarity within the system.

Labeling Octaves and Tones: Nomenclature
*In some countries, **Scientific Pitch Notation (SPN)** is mostly utilized, which involves numerically labeling octaves from **octave 0** (the lowest two notes on a standard keyboard) to **the 8th octave** (the highest tone on a regular piano keyboard). Other countries prefer **Helmholtz Pitch Notation**, which labels the octave as "subcontra," "contra," "great," and "small"—up to the middle C and then "one-line," "two-line," "three-line,"" four-line," and" five-line" labels from middle C up. Clefi is versatile and uses Helmholtz Pitch Notation back home in Czechia and SPN when he's in the USA, like this:*

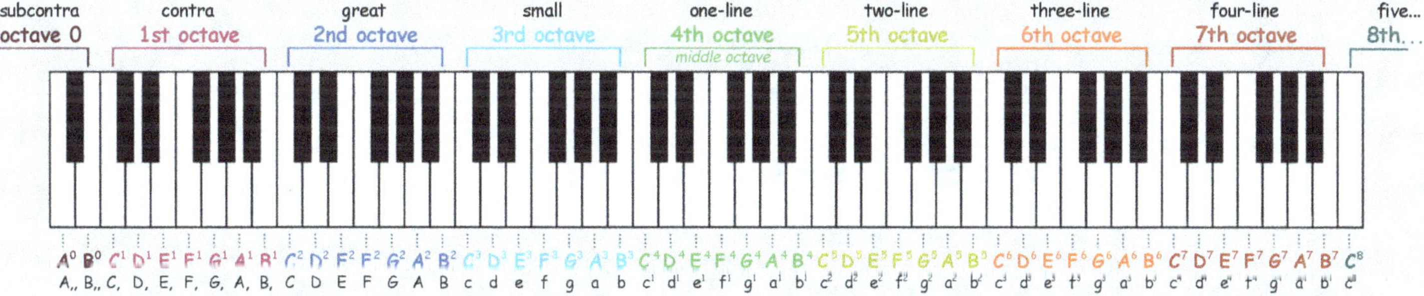

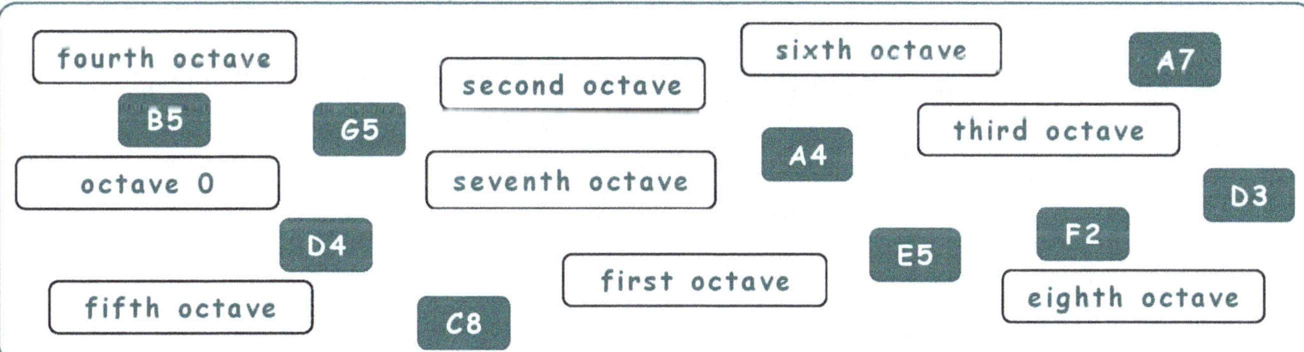

E Link the tones with their appropriate octaves.

MUSICAL NOTATION

Musical notation is a collection of symbols used to write tones.
The most fundamental music notation symbols are **notes**.

CHARACTERISTICS OF MUSICAL NOTES

- **Note Duration:** Represented by the **shape** of the note.
- **Note Pitch:** Determined by the **clef** and the **placement** of the note on the staff.
- **Note Volume:** Indicated by **dynamic symbols** *(dynamics)*.
- **Note Color:** Reflected by the selected **instrument** or **voice**.

In certain notated compositions, you may find descriptions that guide how to play the notes in a way that aligns with the composer's intent, using terms such as "dark" or "harshly."

NOTES & RESTS

A **note** is a musical symbol that represents a sound, while a **rest** is a musical symbol that indicates a period of silence in music. The **shape** of a **note** or **rest** determines its **duration**. Each note and rest has a specific value that represents the **number** of **beats** it lasts.

Fundamental Values of Notes and Rests

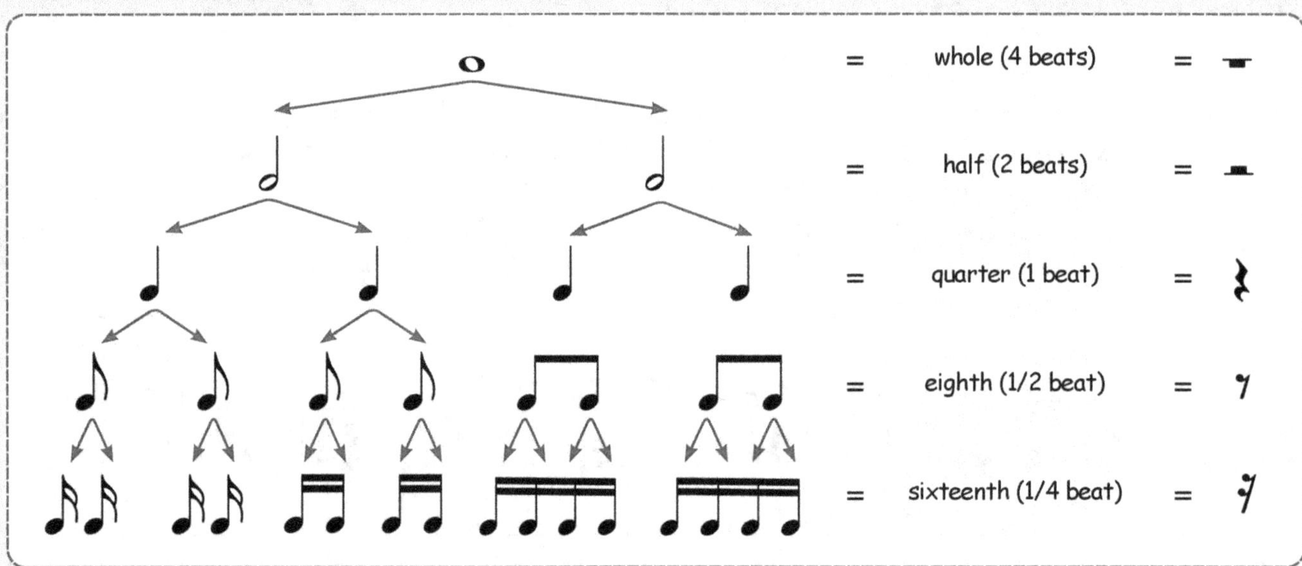

EXTENDING DURATION OF NOTES AND RESTS

- A **dot** placed **after** a **note** or **rest** extends its duration by half of its original value.
- A **tie** is a curved line that connects two notes of the same pitch, combining their values into one. The total duration of all the notes under a tie is added together.
- A **fermata** extends the duration of a note, though the exact number of beats it lasts is not specified. Typically, it adds an extra length equal to half of the note's original value.

dot after note

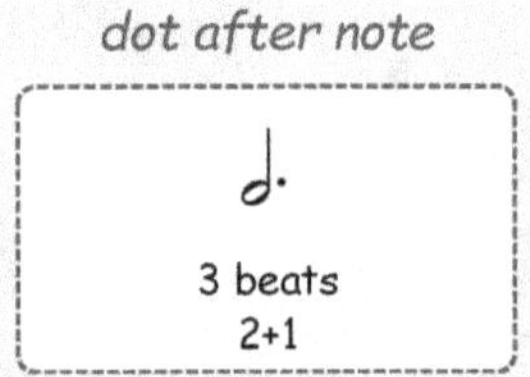

tie

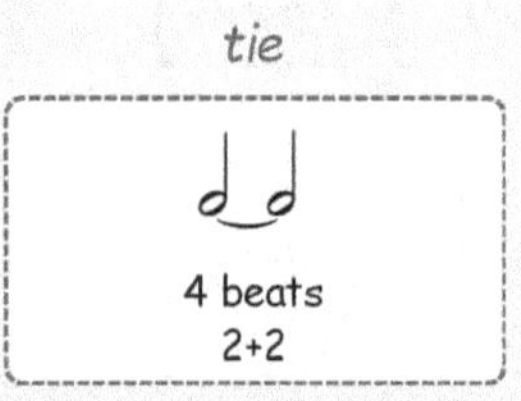

fermata

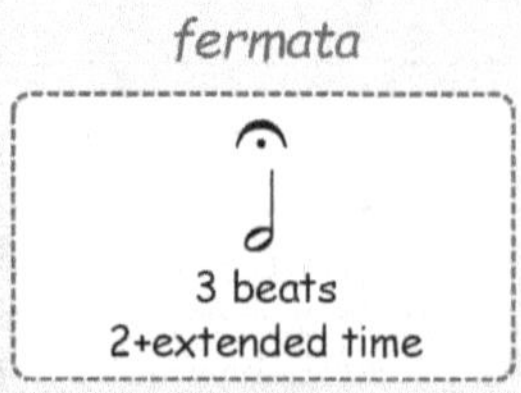

STAFF & CLEF

The pitch of a note is determined by its position on a **musical staff**. A **musical staff** consists of five lines and four spaces. Notes are placed on the lines and in the spaces of the staff. If notes need to be positioned above or below the top or bottom line, we use **ledger lines**.

All notes shorter than a whole note have a **stem**. The stem is placed on the left side of a note down if it is situated in the lower half of the staff (the middle line and down) and on the left side of the note down if it's in the upper half of the staff (the middle line and up). To accommodate instruments with a wide range, we use the **octave transposition symbol** to notate notes that fall outside the range of the ledger lines.

A **clef** determines the note pitch for the entire notation.

COMMON MODERN MUSIC CLEFS

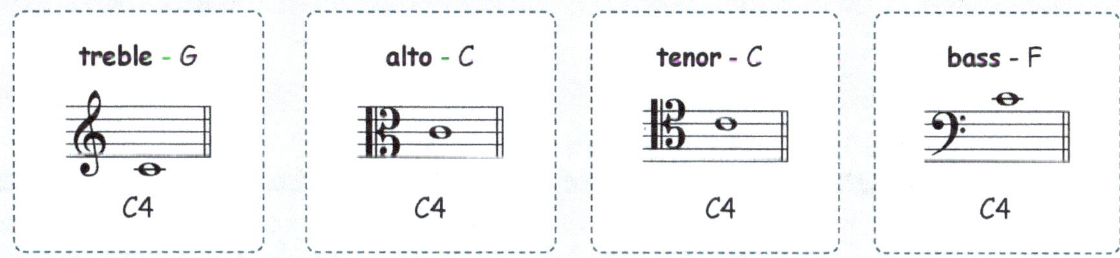

E   Fill the note values in the number of beats into the boxes below each note.

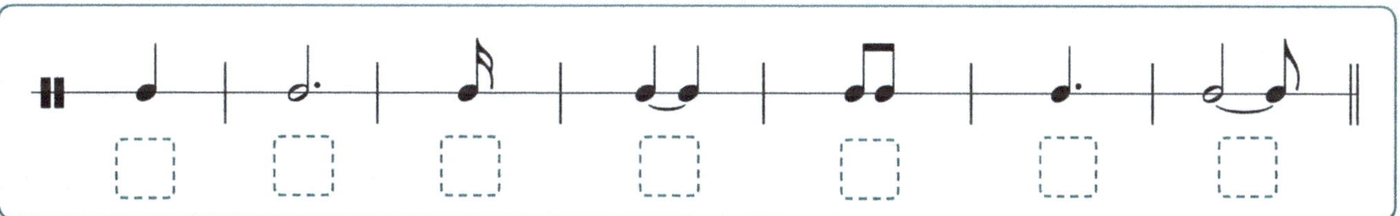

E   Notate half notes according to their names below the staff. Pay attention to the placement of stems. Use the octave transposition symbol for the notes in the 6th and 1st octaves.

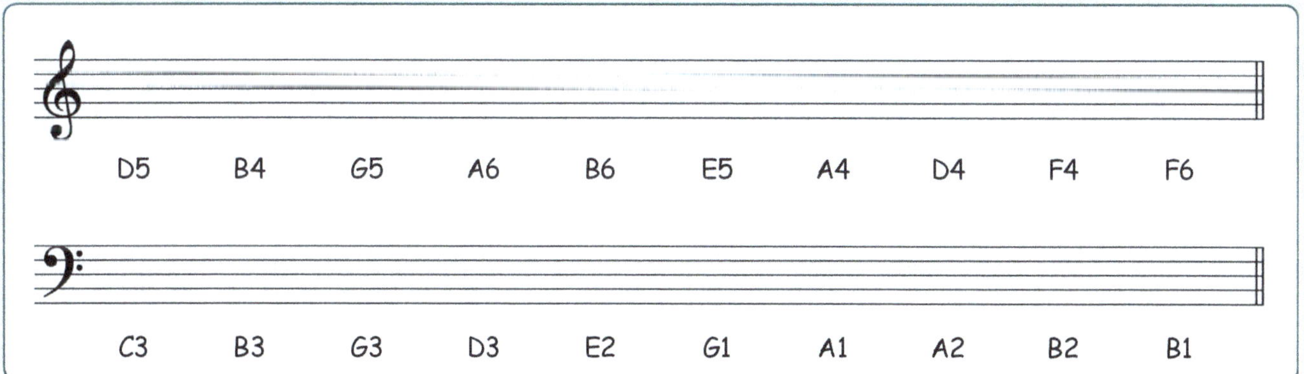

3

RHYTHM, MEASURE

RHYTHM

The word "**rhythm**" originates from the ancient Greek term "**rhythmos**," which means "**flow**." Rhythm can be defined as a regular pattern of motion, sound, or events. For example, our hearts function with a specific rhythm, which we can also observe in our breathing, walking, or dancing.

The **tempo** is a word expressing the **velocity** of regular rhythm (motion). In music, we use tempo terminology to indicate how slow or fast we should play a piece.

The **meter** serves as a rhythmic blueprint, dividing a musical composition into core units that express the organization of heavy and light beats within a measure. In poetry, "meter" similarly orchestrates the flow of words, enriching the emotional depth of the verses.

MEASURES

Measures are short sections of a musical composition that are separated by bar lines. Each measure is further divided into beats. The **time signature**, which consists of two numbers stacked on top of each other, determines the beat division within a measure. The upper number indicates the number of beats per measure, while the lower number represents the note value of each beat. For example, 4/4 and 2/2 measures can also be represented with these symbols: 4/4 - 𝄴, 2/2 - 𝄵 . A **pickup measure**, often referred to simply as a **pickup**, is an **incomplete measure** that appears at the beginning of a composition.

SIMPLE AND COMBINED MEASURES

- A **simple measure** has only one heavy beat. The most common simple measures are 2/2, 3/4, and 3/8.
- A **combined measure** contains multiple beats that can be divided into two or more simple measures. These measures have more than one heavy beat, including a primary **downbeat** and one or more secondary heavy beats. The most common combined measures are 4/4, 6/4, 6/8, and 9/8.
- A combined measure that can be divided into **two or more groups of three beats** is in a **compound meter**.

DIAGRAMS OF FUNDAMENTAL CONDUCTING PATTERNS

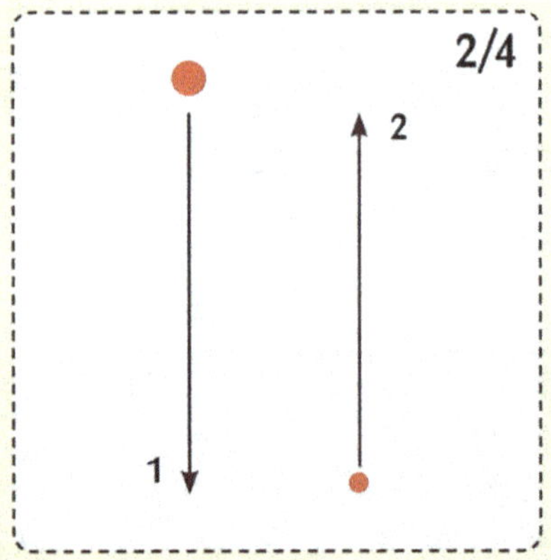

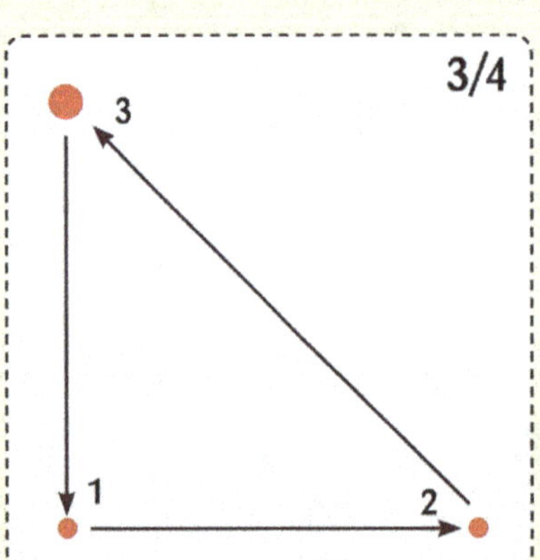

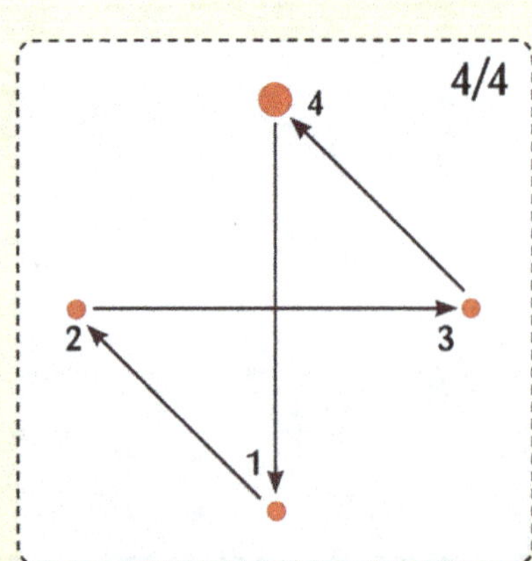

RHYTHMIC PATTERNS

A rhythmic pattern is a group of notes. Rhythmic patterns usually observe the rhythmic structure of a composition, meaning they maintain the established beat sequence. However, we can encounter a rhythmic pattern that deviates from the main rhythmic structure of a composition. For example, syncopation alters the primary accent of an initial rhythmic pattern.

Most Common Rhythmic Patterns

- **Syncopation** involves **transferring an accent** from the heavy beat to the light beat.
- A **dotted rhythm** is named after a dotted note and rhythm created by alternating between dotted longer and regular shorter notes.
- **Duplets**, **triplets**, **quadruplets**, and **quintuplets** are rhythmic patterns created by subdividing a beat into equal parts that fall outside the regular subdivisions determined by the meter. Specifically, duplets consist of two parts, triplets of three parts, quadruplets of four parts, quintuplets of five parts, and so on.

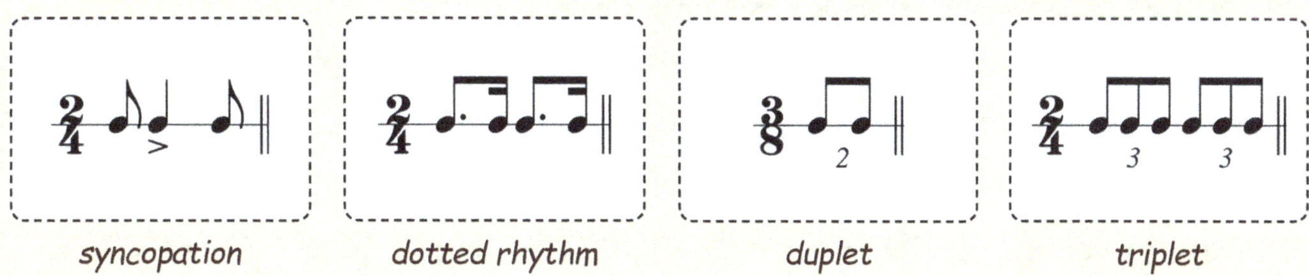

syncopation   dotted rhythm   duplet   triplet

E Fill in the measure lines according to the time signatures, then clap the rhythm.

E Connect the boxes that belong together.

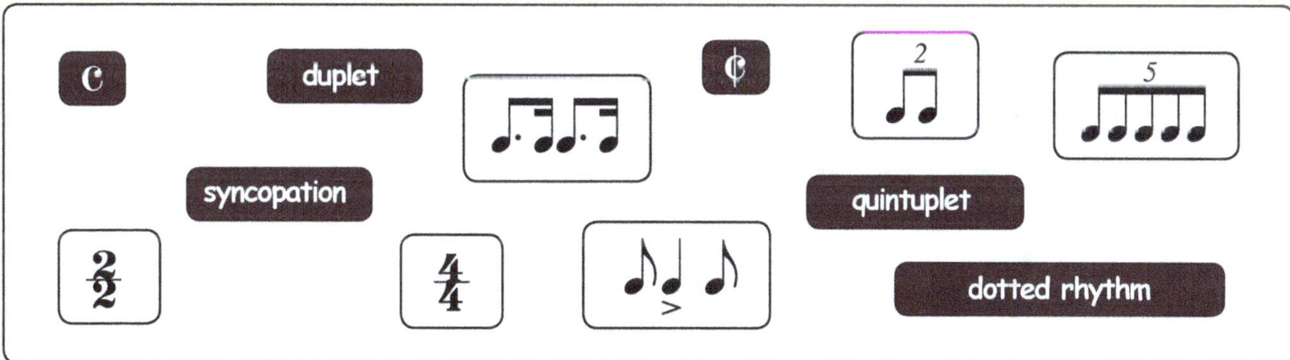

ACCIDENTALS, ENHARMONIC TONES

Primary tones serve as the foundation of the **primary tone row**: C-D-E-F-G-A-B. **Altered tones** are created by **raising** or **lowering** the primary tones using musical symbols known as **accidentals**. An accidental remains in effect for the entire measure in which it is applied.

Commonly Used Accidentals:

♯ **a sharp** - raises a tone by a half step

♭ **a flat** - lowers a tone by a half step

✖ **a double sharp** - raises a tone by two half steps (a whole step)

♭♭ **a double flat** - lowers a tone by two half steps (a whole step)

♮ **a natural** - cancels all accidentals and key signature sharps and flats

ENHARMONIC TONES

Enharmonically exchangeable tones are tones that sound the same but have different names. Each pitch can be notated in several ways because there are **twelve distinct pitches** within an octave, but **35 different notes** in total. These include **seven primary tones**, each of which can be altered in four ways: for example, **C** is primary, and **C♯**, **Cx**, **C♭**, and **C♭♭** are altered.

Example:

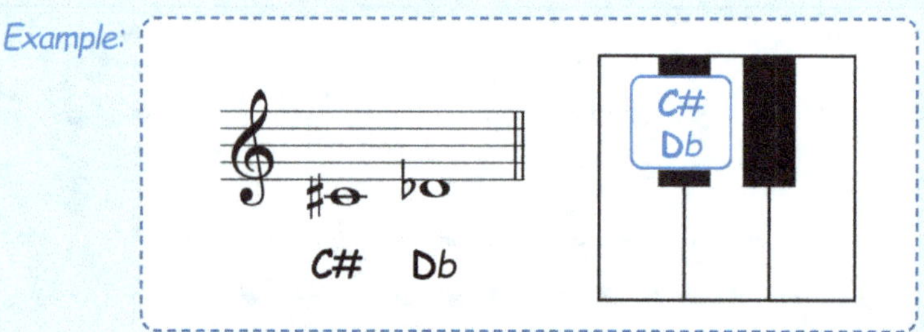

E Write the names of the notes in the boxes below. Pay attention to the accidentals and their duration. Add stems to create half notes.

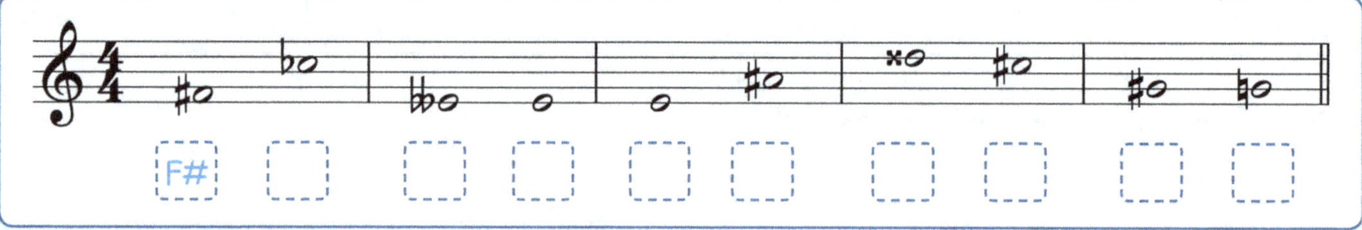

E Notate enharmonically exchanged notes into the boxes next to each note.

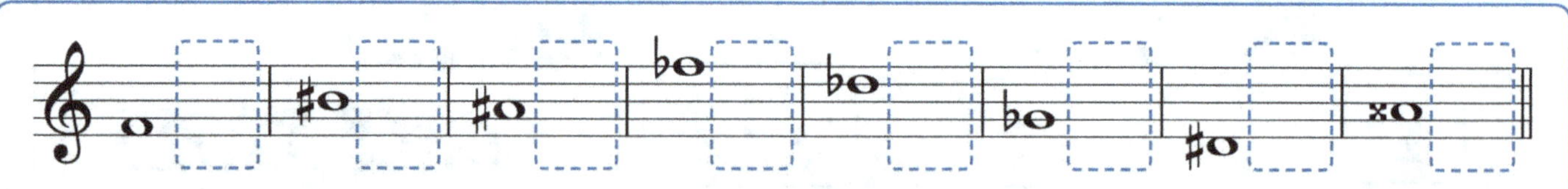

INTERVALS

A **musical interval** is a pitch difference between two tones.

The full name of musical intervals consists of two parts: the interval's **numeric label** (number) and its **quality**. The intervals' **numeric labels** (numbers) are: **unison** (1st), **second** (2nd), **third** (3rd), **fourth** (4th), **fifth** (5th), **sixth** (6th), **seventh** (7th) and **octave** (8th). These names are derived from differences between tones of a primary tone row.

The **interval quality** specifies its exact range. The five primary interval qualities are: **perfect**, **major**, **minor**, **augmented**, and **diminished**. Since we have twelve tones but only eight numeric labels, the use of the interval quality label is essential for all intervals. For example, saying simply "third" does not describe the exact distance between two tones. The primary third is a major third (the distance of four half steps), the first altered third is a minor third (distance of three half steps), and both can be further augmented or diminished.

Upper & Lower Intervals

- The upper intervals are intervals measured from the lower note to the higher.
- The lower intervals are intervals measured from the higher note to the lower.

Melodic & Harmonic Intervals

- The melodic intervals are intervals played in succession as a melody.
- The harmonic interval are intervals played simultaneously, creating a harmony.

E Notate the intervals from the assigned notes. Pay attention to the orange arrows that indicate whether to create upper or lower intervals.

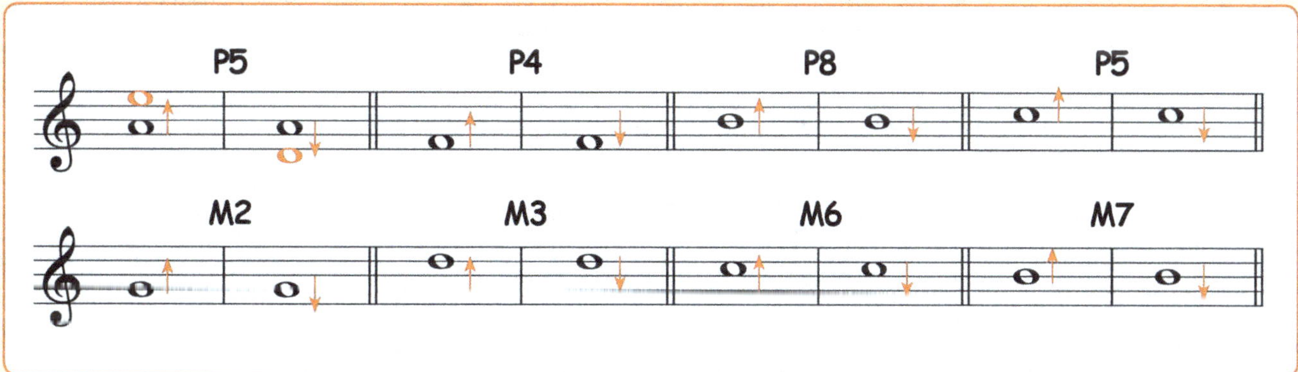

E Connect boxes that belong together. Circle the melodic intervals.

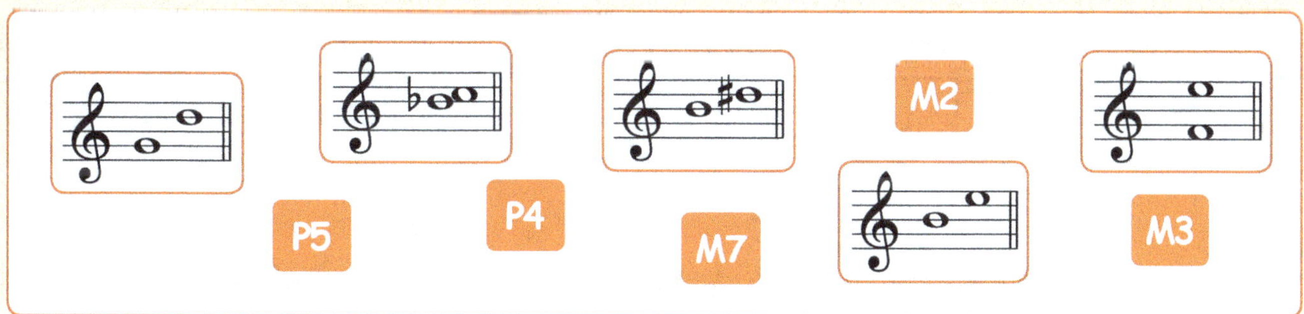

INTERVAL CLASSIFICATION

Primary intervals and intervals between the tones of any major scale.
These primary intervals are classified as **perfect** and **major**.

Perfect Intervals: the unison, fourth, fifth, and octave

- Perfect intervals are the first, fourth, fifth, and eighth degrees of all diatonic scales.
- Altered perfect intervals are diminished (a half step smaller than a perfect interval) and augmented (a half step bigger than a perfect interval).

Major Intervals: the second, third, sixth, and seventh.

- Major intervals are the second, third, sixth, and seventh degrees of all major scales. All other diatonic scales feature major and minor intervals on their 2nd, 3rd, 6th, and 7th degrees, according to their modes.
- Altered major intervals are minor (a half step smaller than a major interval), diminished (a half step smaller than a minor interval), and augmented (a half step bigger than a major interval).

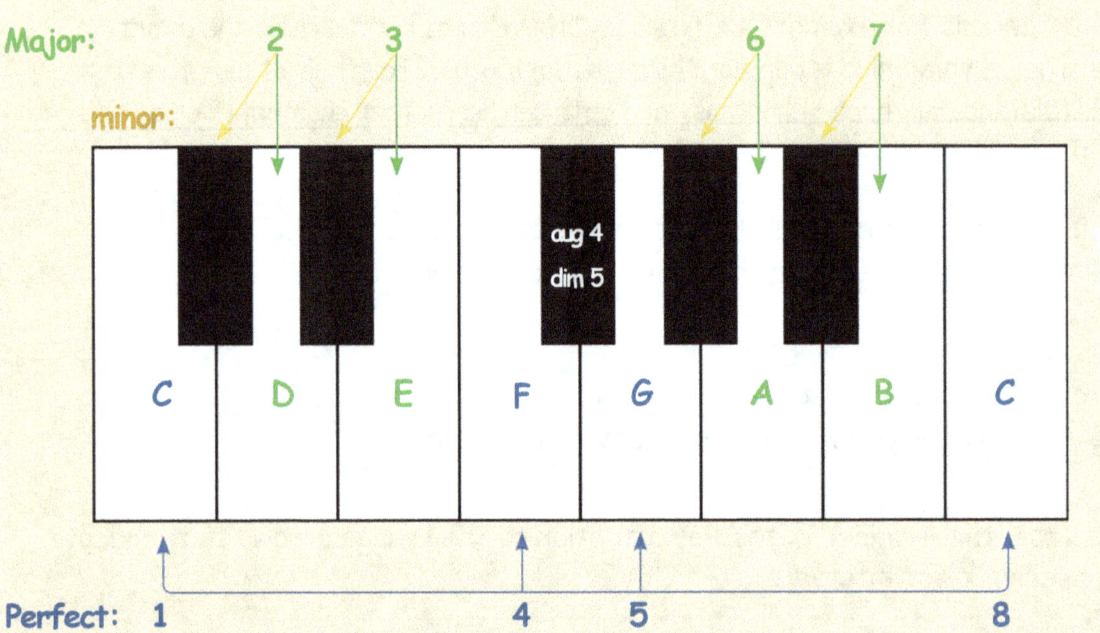

E   Notate all primary intervals from the note D4. Circle the perfect ones.

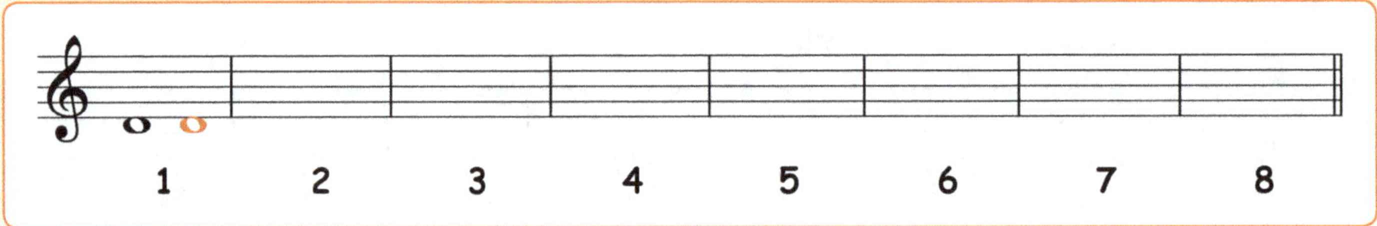

E   Lable the altered intervals into the boxes below the staff.

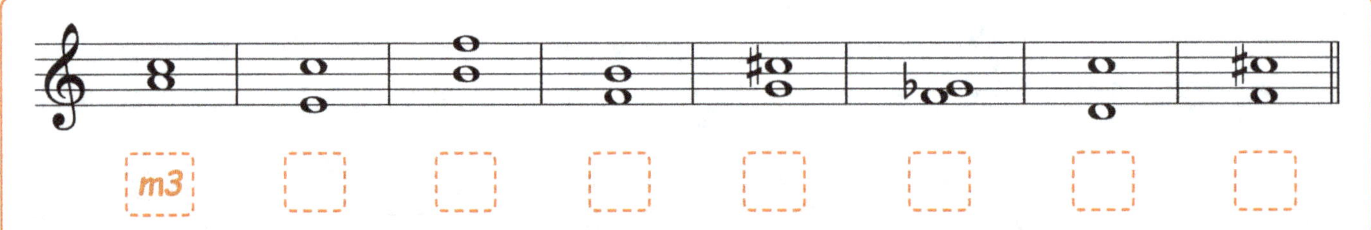

INTERVAL INVERSIONS

Interval inversions are created by moving the rot of the interval an octave higher or by moving the top not of the interval an octave lower. With this move we get a different, specific interval.

- By **inverting** a **perfect interval**, we always get another **perfect interval**: P1 becomes P8, P4 becomes P5, P5 becomes P4, P8 becomes P1.
- By **inverting** a **major interval**, we always get a **minor interval**: M2 becomes m7, M3 becomes m6, M6 becomes m3, and M7 becomes m2. The same but inverted rule applies to inverting the first alterations of the major intervals when minor intervals become major (m2 becomes M7 and so on).

Interesting fact for music math lovers:
The sum of intervals and their inversions is always 9: 1 + 8 = 9, 4 + 5 = 9, 2 + 7 = 9, and 3 + 6 = 9.

Interval Inversions:

COMMON INTERVALS LARGER THAN OCTAVE

- 9th (ninth) = 8th (octave) + 2nd (second)
- 10th (tenth) = 8th (octave) + 3rd (third)
- 11th (eleventh) = 8th (octave) + 4th (fourth)
- 12th (twelfth) = 8th (octave) + 5th (fifth)
- 13th (thirteeenth) = 8th (octave) + 6th (sixth)

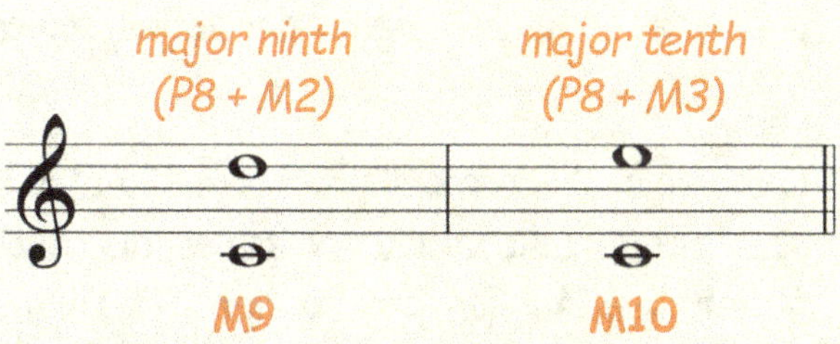

When we move the upper tone of an interval up or the lower one down by an octave or more, we get a **transferred interval**. The name and quality of the transferred interval remain unchanged. For example, a second remains a second, and a perfect interval remains perfect.

Transfered Intervals:

Notate the interval inversions in the boxes next to them.

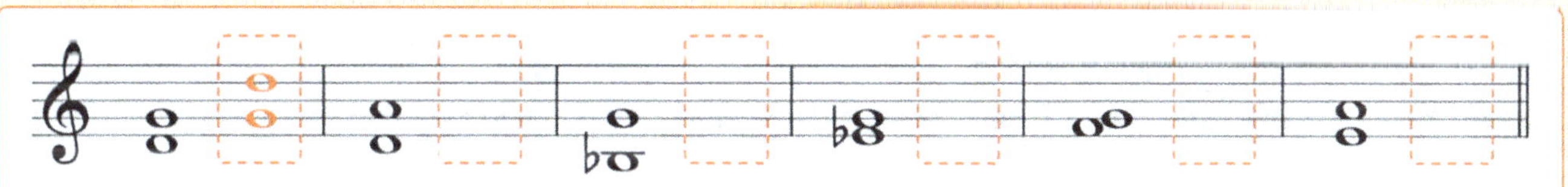

Circle the correct examples.

TYPES OF SCALES

A **scale** is a row of tones within **one octave** arranged according to specific rules. These rules govern the **number of tones** in the scale and the size of the **intervals between them**.

The **number of tones** is **fixed** for all types of scales. Each scale begins and ends with the same tone, separated by an octave. Scales can contain **five**, **six**, **seven**, or **twelve tones**.

*The number of distinct tones in a scale refers to the **different, not the repeated tones**. The repeated tones are not reflected in the characterization. For example, the C major scale has seven different tones, C-D-E-F-G-A-B. The last repeated tone C is the same as the first one (regardless of an octave difference); therefore, the C major scale is the **seven-tone scale**.*

COMMON TYPES OF SCALES

One of the most essential rules of building scales is the **distances between the tones**. These distances determine the **structure of a scale** (half steps, whole steps, and one-and-a-half steps). Based on the distances between neighboring tones, scales can be classified as **diatonic**, **chromatic**, **whole tone**, or **exotic**.

Diatonic Scales

Diatonic scales are built from **whole (1)** and **half steps (1/2)**. Diatonic scales include **modern major** and **minor** scales and **medieval church** scales, also known as **ancient Greek** scales, such as **Dorian**, **Phrygian**, **Lydian**, **Mixolydian**, **Aeolian**, and **Locrian**. *(The major scale is also known by its ancient Greek name as **Ionian**.)*

Chromatic Scales

Chromatic scales are built solely from **half steps (1/2)**.

Whole-Tone Scales

The whole-tone scales are built solely from **whole steps (1)**.

Exotic Scales

Exotic scales have an **unusual step structure** and produce a sound that may seem intriguing and exotic to those of us trained in Western music. Examples of exotic scales include the **pentatonic** scales, which are constructed using **whole steps (1)** and **one-and-a-half steps $(1, 1\frac{1}{2})$**, and **gypsy** scales, which are made up of **half steps (1/2)**, **whole steps (1)**, and **one-and-a-half $(1, 1\frac{1}{2})$ steps**.

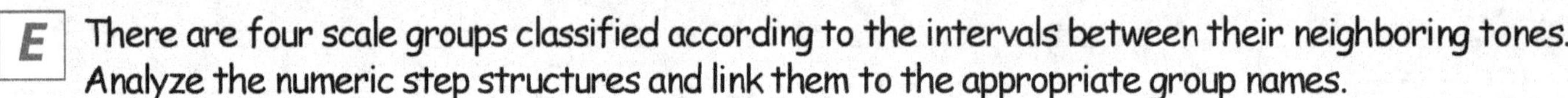

E There are four scale groups classified according to the intervals between their neighboring tones. Analyze the numeric step structures and link them to the appropriate group names.

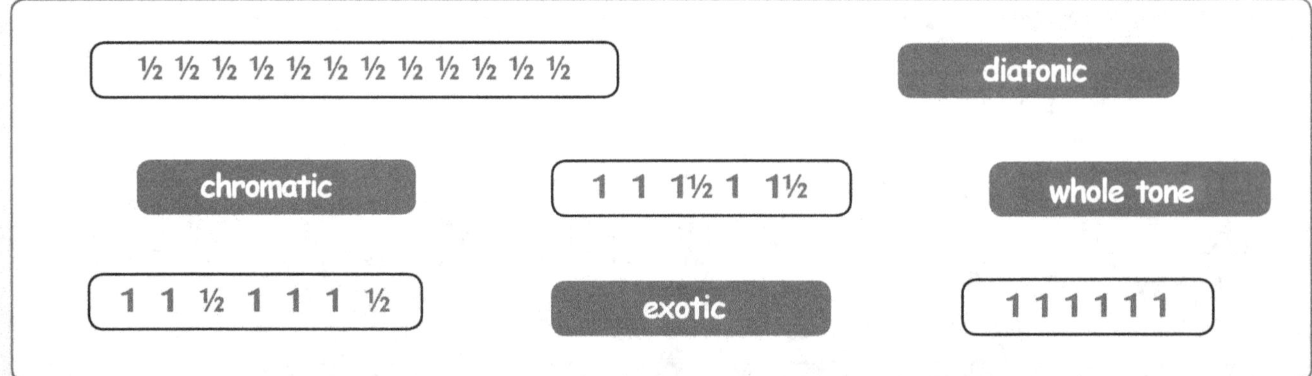

DIATONIC SCALES

Diatonic scales are most commonly used scales in Western music. Diatonic scales included **modern** major and minor and the **old church** (ancient Greek) scale.

MAIN CHARACTERISTICS OF DIATONIC SCALES

- **Seven-tone Scales:** The row of seven different tones (root and arrival tones are the same)
- Contain **whole** and **half steps**.
- Diatonic scales included **modern** and **old church** also known as **ancient Greek** scales.
- **Primary diatonic scales** are built from the tones of the primary tone row.
  - modern: **major** - C major, **minor** - A minor
  - old church: **C Ionian, D Dorian, E Phrygian, F Lydian, G Mixolydian, A Aeolian,** *B Locrian**
- All primary diatonic scales have **seven additional sharp** and **seven additional flat scales**.

Primary Diatonic Scales Overview

modern scales		old church (ancient Greek) scales
C-D-E-F-G-A-B-C - major	=	Ionian: C-D-E-F-G-A-B-C
		Dorian: D-E-F-G-A-B-C-D
		Phrygian: E-F-G-A-B-C-D-E
		Lydian: F-G-A-B-C-D-E-F
		Mixolydian: G-A-B-C-D-E-F-G
A-B-C-D-E-F-G-A - minor	=	Aeolian: A-B-C-D-E-F-G-A
		Locrian: B-C-D-E-F-G-A-B

major / Ionian
Dorian
Phrygian
Lydian
Mixolydian
natural minor / Aeolian
Locrian*

*All diatonic scales are built from the tones of the primary tone row. We have seven primary tones, resulting in seven diatonic scales. *However, the seventh scale, Locrian, was effectively deemed forbidden during the Renaissance period because it was perceived as too dissonant, due to its diminished fifth chord and overall tense nature.*

E   Write the names of the scales that correspond to major and minor scales.
Color the boxes with the modern scales in green.

major	=	__________		minor	=	__________

MODERN MAJOR & MINOR SCALES

Modern **major** and **minor scales** are the most commonly used scales in music today.

Major scales have a major mode, which sounds open, upbeat, and happy. Their primary characteristic is the major third. The musical symbol for major scales is an uppercase letter representing the scale's key - "C."
Minor scales have a minor mode, which gives them a melancholy and sad sound. Their main characteristic is the minor third interval. The musical symbol for a minor scale consists of an uppercase letter for the scale key, followed by a lowercase "m" - "Am."

Primary and Derived Scales
* The **primary major** scale is **C major** (only primary tones, no key signature).
  The **primary minor** scale is **A minor** (only primary tones, no key signature).
* **Derived scales:**

major:	seven scales with sharps: $G, D, A, E, B, F^{\#}, C^{\#}$	seven scales with flats: $F, B^b, E^b, A^b, D^b, G^b, C^b$
minor:	seven scales with sharps: $Em, Bm, F^{\#}m, C^{\#}m, G^{\#}, D^{\#}, A^{\#}m$	seven scales with flats: $Dm, Gm, Cm, Fm, B^bm, E^bm, A^bm$

Major and **minor scales** might share **similar traits:**
* **relative scales** - the same key signature
* **parallel scales** - the same root tone - the given name

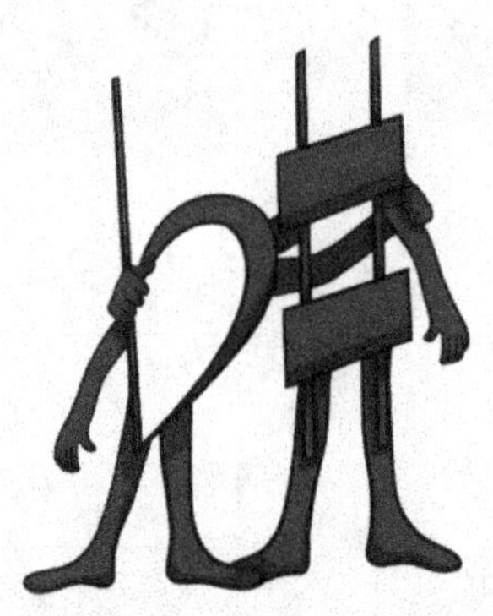

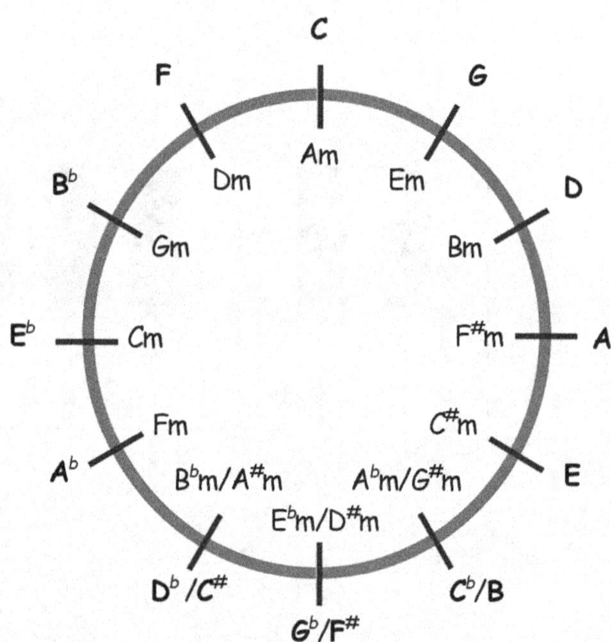

Sharps and flats are added in the same order in both major and minor scales.
The order of sharps in the key signatures: F#, C#, G#, D#, A#, E#, B#
The order of flats in the key signature: Bb, Eb, Ab, Db, Gb, Cb, Fb

E	Notate the sharps and flats on the separate staffs in order as they progress through the key signatures.

Enharmonic scales are two different scales that sound the same but are notated differently.
They have **enharmonically interchangeable root tones**, meaning each scale has a **different name**.

Major Eharmonic Scales	the magical no. 12	Minor Enharmonic Scales
B major = C^b major	5 sharps = 7 flats	$G^\#$ minor = A^b minor
$F^\#$ major = G^b major	6 sharps = 6 flats	$D^\#$ minor = E^b minor
$C^\#$ major = D^b major	7 sharps = 5 flats	$A^\#$ minor = B^b minor

E
1. Notate the assigned major scales and their relative minor.
2. Notate the assigned minor scales and their parallel major.

E
- Indicate the number of accidentals above the scale symbols provided.
- Use blue to link the scales with sharps in the order they appear on the Circle of Fifths.
- Use green to link the scales with flats in the order they appear on the Circle of Fifths.
- Color the enharmonic scales using a color of your choice.

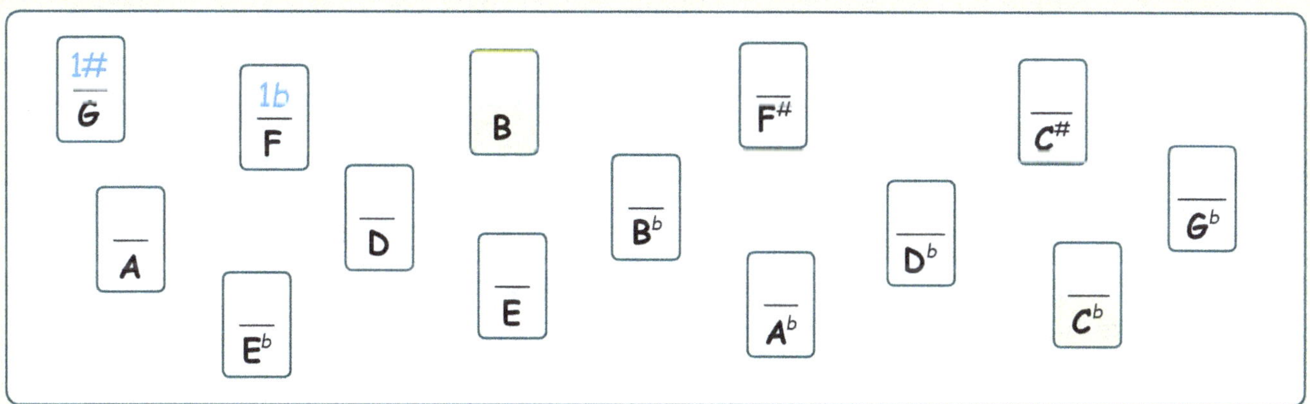

OLD CHURCH SCALES

Old church scales originated in Europe and the Middle East during the ancient Greek period, which is reflected in their Greek names. In medieval times, these scales (*except for the Locrian, which was excluded by the church for its highly dissonant character*) were primarily used in churches for religious music, which is why they are known as **old church scales** or **modes**.

Primary Old Church Scales Scales

- All scales are built on the **tones** of the **primary tone row:**
- **C - Ionian, D - Dorian, E - Phrygian, F - Lydian, G - Mixolydian, A - Aeolian,** *B - Locrian*

The Ionian scale is the major scale, and the Aeolian scale is the modern natural minor scale. The Locrian scale is rarely used. In this book, we will focus on the four favorite old church scales.

Dorian Scale
- starts on the **second degree** of a major scale
- a **minor mode** (m3)
- the characteristic interval - **M6 (Dorian sixth)**

Phrygian Scale
- starts on the third **degree** of a major scale
- a **minor mode** (m3)
- the characteristic interval - **m2 (Phrygian second)**

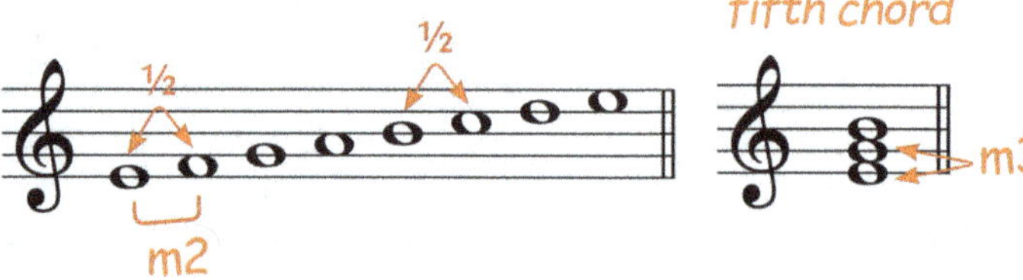

Lydian scale
- starts on the **fourth degree** of a major scale
- a **major mode** (M3)
- the characteristic interval - **A4 (Lydian fourth)**

Mixolydian scale
- starts on the **fifth degree** of a major scale
- a **major mode** (M3)
- the characteristic interval - **m7 (Mixolydian seventh)**

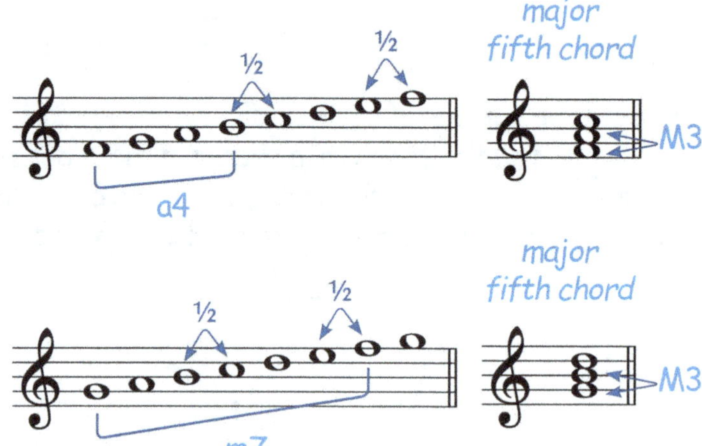

These are the primary forms of the old church scales. We can derive seven sharp and seven flat scales from all of these, similar to how we do with modern major and minor scales.

Relative Diatonic Scales

Relative scales have the same key signature.
Old church scales are derived from their **relative major scales**.

- **Primary diatonic scales** with no key signature are built on the tones of the **primary major scale**, C major.
- All **other diatonic scales with sharps** or **flats** are built from the tones of **other sharp** or **flat major scales** with which they **share the key signature**.

Example: 3 sharps = A major: **A-B-C#-D-E-F#-G#-A**
B Dorian: **B-C#-D-E-F#-G#-A-B**
C# Phrygian: **C#-D-E-F#-G#-A-B-C#**
D Lydian: **D-E-F#-G#-A-B-C#-D**
E Mixolydian: **E-F#-G#-A-B-C#-D-E**
F# Aeolian: **F#-G#-A-B-C#-D-E-F#**
G# Locrian: **G#-A-B-C#-D-E-F#-G#**

E | Notate the D major scale = D Ionian. Write the name of the note on the line below the staff. The relative diatonic scales with the identical key signatures start on the degrees of this scale. Notate the relative Dorian and Phrygian scales to D major. Indicate the root tone in the boxes next to the names.

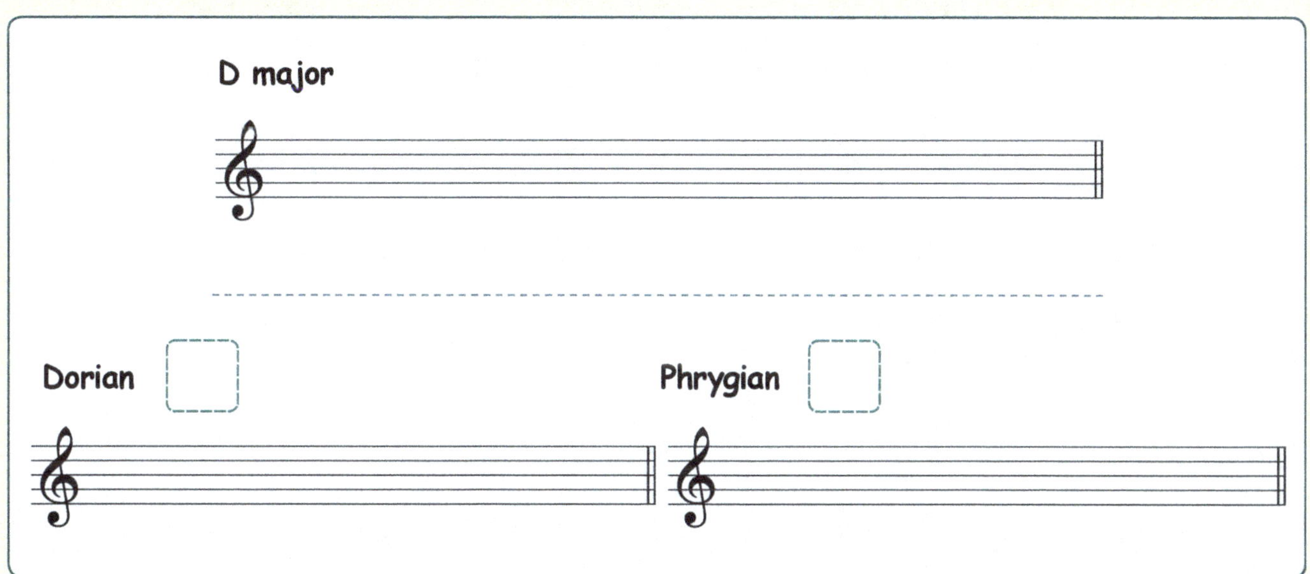

E | Complete the table.

scale name	key mode (the third)	characteristic interval
Dorian	*minor (m3)*	*M6*
Phrygian		
Lydian		
Mixolydian		

The Influence of Old Church Modes on Central European Folk Songs

Old church modes have had a profound impact on the folk music of Central Europe. Here are some examples of songs that showcase the four most popular old church modes. Each song is first presented in the primary old church mode scale derived from the primary C major scale, and then with the note C as the root degree, allowing you to observe the key signature of its relative major scale.

Parsley, Sage, Mint, Bit of Basil *(Dorian)*
Clefi & Notelina's Songbook page 89

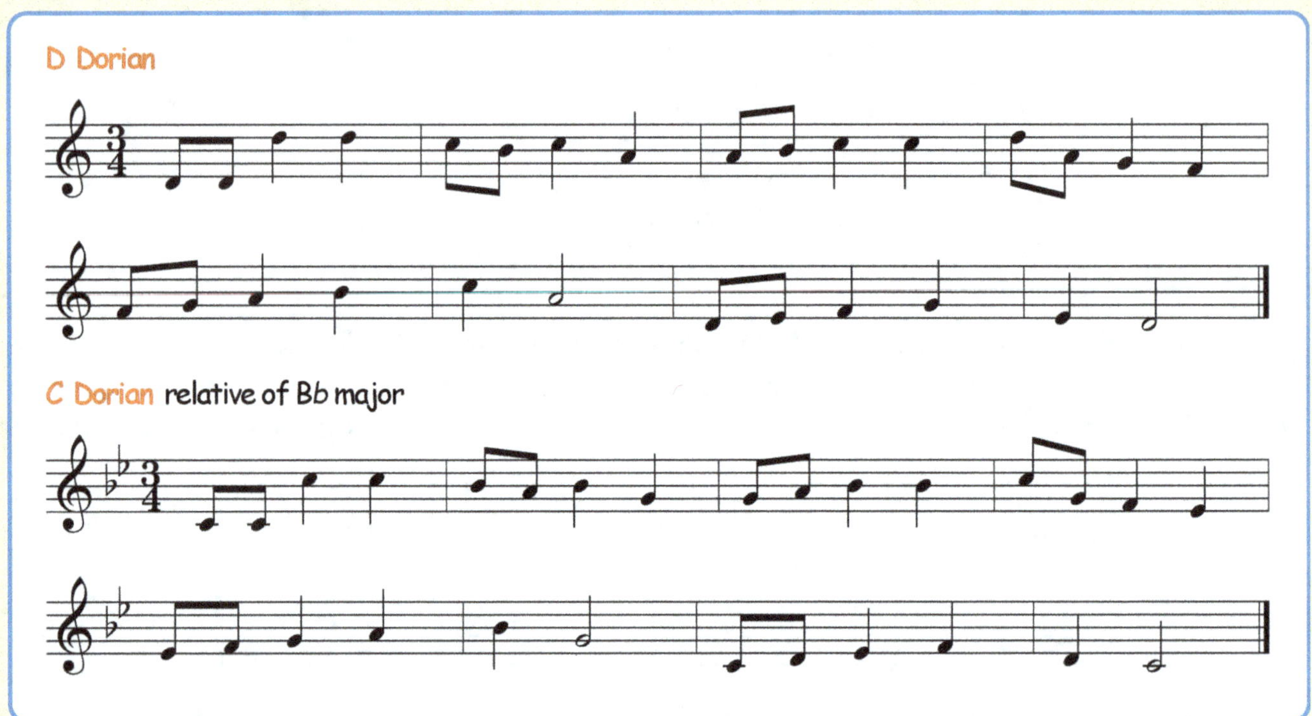

Wars Have Happened This Year *(Phrygian)*
Clefi & Notelina's Songbook page 90

A Little Cuckoo Bird is Calling *(Lydian)*
Clefi and Notelina's Songbook page 91

When I Was at My Mom's Place *(Mixolydian)*
Clefi and Notelina's Songbook page 92

CHROMATIC & WHOLE-TONE SCALES

Chromatic and **whole-tone scales** are distinct from other scales as they have **consistent intervals** between neighboring tones. A **chromatic** scale consists solely of **half steps**, while a **whole-tone** scale is made up entirely of **whole steps**.

CHROMATIC SCALE

The main characteristics are as follows:

- A **twelve-tone scale** - a row of twelve tones within one octave.
- It contains only **half steps** between neighboring tones.
- Uses **sharps while ascending** and **flats while descending**.

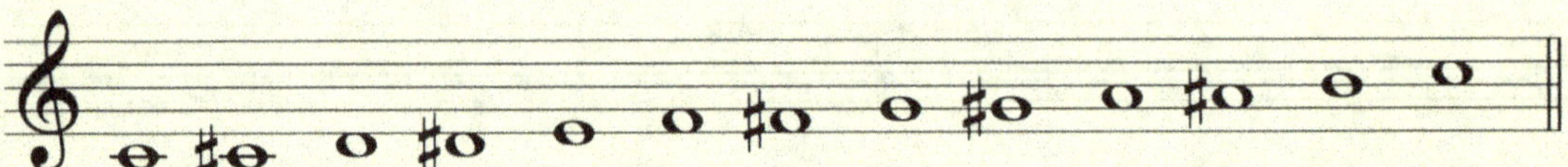

WHOLE-TONE SCALE

The main characteristics are as follows:

- A **six-tone scale** - a row of six tones within one octave.
- It contains only **whole steps** between neighboring tones.
- The seventh tone is the root tone. When progressing by major seconds, we have to enharmonically exchange the seventh note to preserve the octave boundaries of a scale like this: C-D-E-F#-G#-A#-(B#)=C.

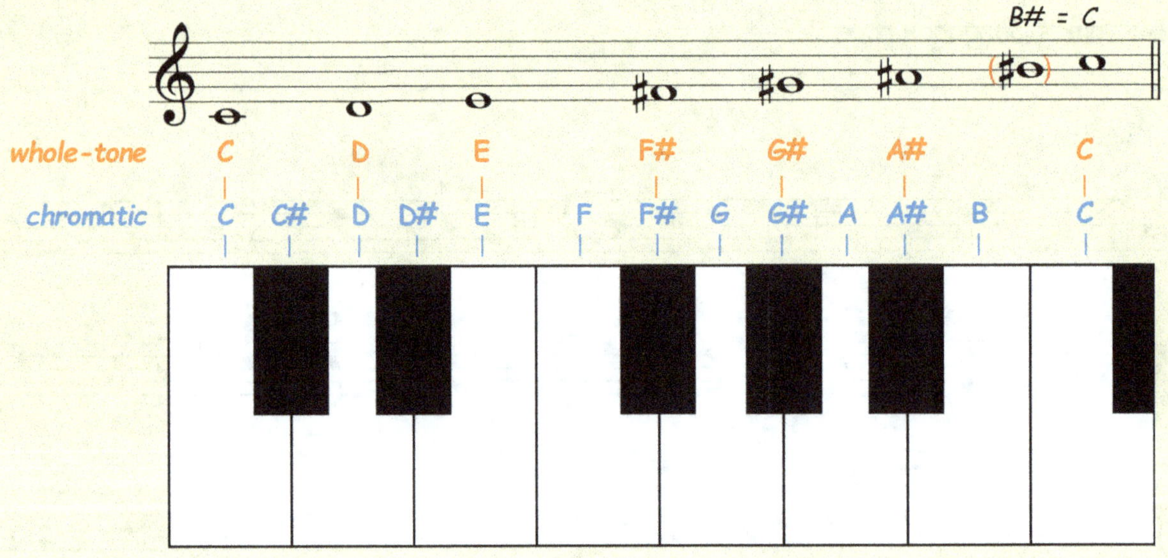

E   Fill in the missing tones for both scales. Write the names of the scales on the dashed lines.

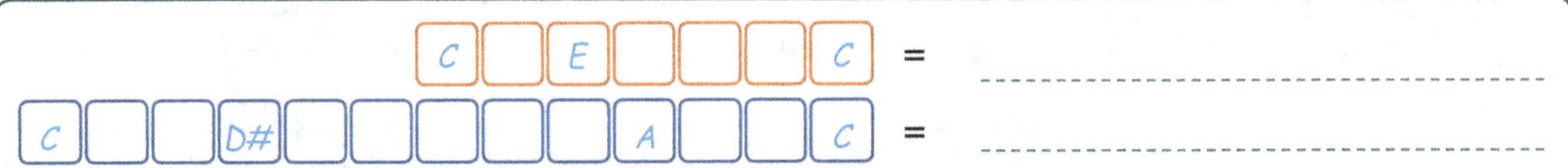

EXOTIC SCALES

Exotic scales include **pentatonic**, **Romani (Gypsy)**, and various other scales outside of common Western music practices, as well as scales constructed according to unique, alternative rules (*for example a scale with the octave divided into 22 parts*).

PENTATONIC SCALE

The main characteristics are as follows:
- A **five-tone** scale (*penta = five*) - a row of five tones within one octave.
- It contains only **whole** and **one and a half steps** between neighboring tones.
- It's possibly the **oldest scale**. It was used during the 3rd millennium BC in the Near East, spreading to Asia, Africa, and even Europe. It's still part of the musical tradition all over Asia.

Even though the pentatonic scale is only major (M3 in the root position) and can be created starting from any of the twelve tones using the step structure as shown above, it can be inverted and used from any of its tones. Most commonly used is the fourth inversion (pentatonic minor - m3) starting on the fifth degree of the major pentatonic scale.

ROMANI (GYPSY) SCALES

The main characteristics are as follows:
- A **seven-tone** scale - same as diatonic scales.
- It contains only **half, whole** and **one and a half steps** between neighboring tones.
- Most common are **double harmonic major** (M3) and **Hungarian (double harmonic) minor** (m3).

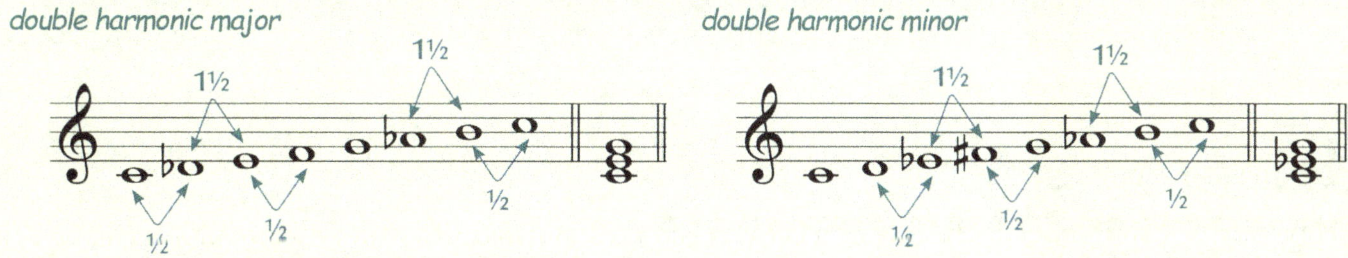

| **E** | Number the steps between the notes (1/2, 1, or 1½). Write the name of the scales on the lines below. |

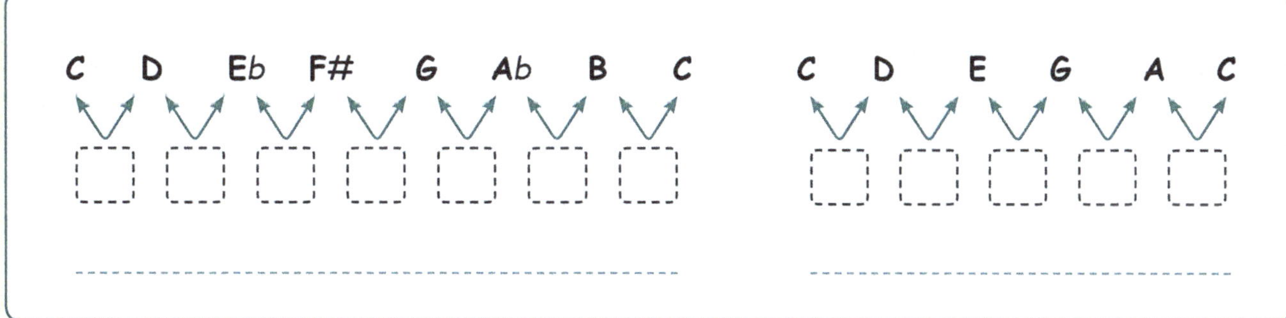

KEY, CHORD

KEY

A **key** defines the relationship of the tone of a composition to a specific scale.
A **quality** defines the character of a key. Major quality = M3 or minor quality = m3.

CHORD

A **chord** is a cluster of three or more tones.

- The most common chord in its **root position** is a fifth chord.
- A **chord inversion** is the chord with the inverted order of its tones.
  Inversions are created by moving the bottom tone an octave higher.

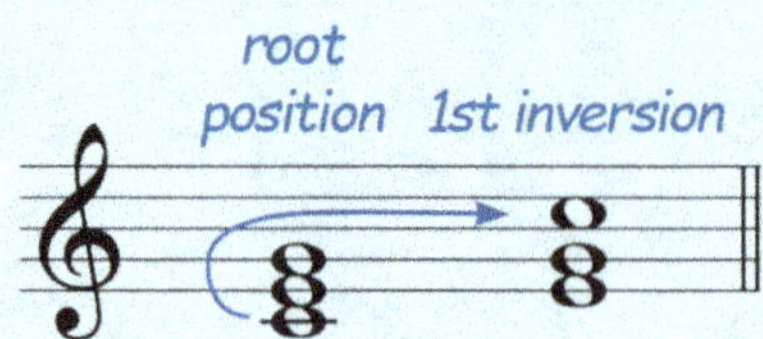

A **chord symbol** is the **abbreviation** used to **label** a **chord**. It contains the chord's **root tone**, its **quality**, and **extensions/alterations**.

Chord Symbol Structure:

- *chord's **root tone** = uppercase letter*
- *chord's major **quality** = uppercase letter alone (C) or uppercase letter followed by uppercase letter "M" or abbreviation "Maj" (CM or CMaj); chord's minor, diminished, and augmented **quality** = uppercase letter followed by lowercase "m" (Cm), "dim" or the symbol "°" (Cdim or C°), "aug" or symbol "+" (Caug or C+)*
- *chord's **extension** and **alteration**: a fifth chord = 5 or nothing; seventh chord = 7; ninth chord = 9; etc. plus symbols for dim, aug, etc.*

root tone - Cm^7 - extension
- quality

HARMONIC FUNCTIONS

Harmonic functions are chords built on the scale's degrees.
Primary harmonic functions:
Tonic = 1st degree; Subdominant = 4th degree; Dominant = 5th degree

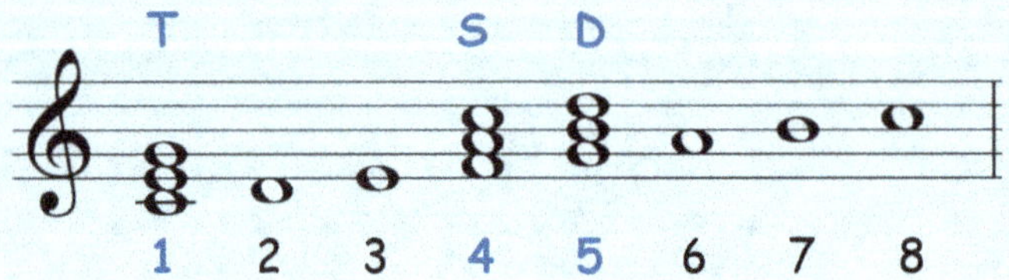

The designations of these harmonic functions (T, S, D) refer to specific degrees of a scale, regardless of the pitch or key.

TYPES OF CHORDS

Chords can be categorized into several groups according to their structure or the number of tones they contain. Two main groups are **fifth chords** (triads) and their first extensions, the **seventh chords** (four-note chords). The most widely used larger extended chords are the **ninth chords** (five-note chords).

The **most common chords** are **constructed** using intervals of **thirds**, known as **tertian** chords. The name of the chord is determined by the intervals between the outer tones, which define its **characteristic interval**.

FIFTH CHORD

A **fifth chord** is a **triad** characterized by the interval of a **fifth (5)**. It consists of a **root**, a **third**, and a **fifth** = **two thirds** on top of each other.

SEVENTH CHORD

A **seventh** chord is a **four-note chord** defined by the interval of a **seventh (7)**. It includes a **fifth chord** and a **seventh** = **three thirds** on top of each other.

NINTH CHORD

A **ninth** chord is a five-note chord characterized by the interval of a **ninth (9)**. It is made up of a **seventh chord** plus an additional **ninth** = **four thirds** on top of each other.

E Identify the types of chords in the exercises: fifth, seventh, or ninth chords. Brace the outer tones of each chord and number the intervals between them according to the example. Then link the chords with the correct designation.

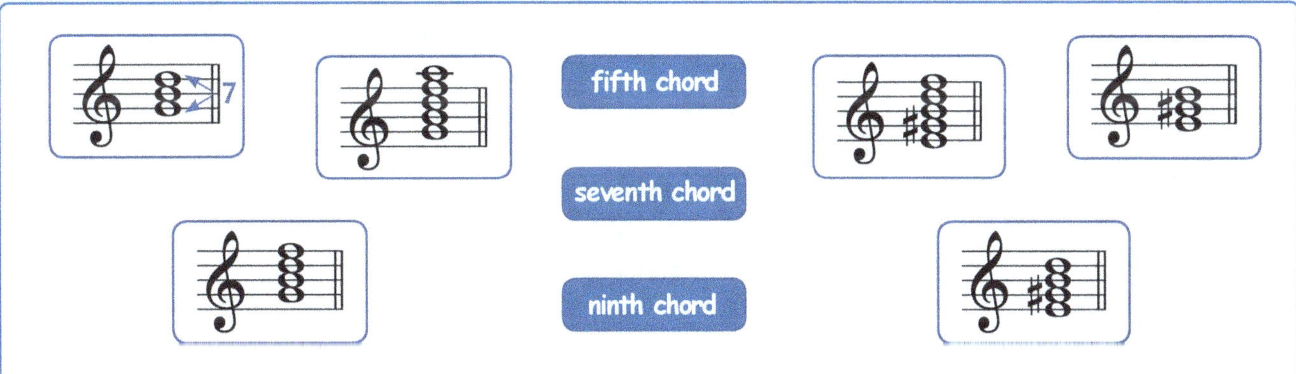

E Fill in the missing fact.

The key's character is called ....

.... is a triad with characteristic interval of a fifth.

To identify the root tone of the chord while labeling it, we use ....

The seventh chord has .... notes and it's .... extension of the fifth chord.

Tonic, ..., and .... are primary harmonic functions.

MAJOR & MINOR FIFTH CHORD

ROOT POSITIONS

The **interval** between the outer tones of **major** and **minor fifth chords** is a **perfect fifth**. These chords **differ** in their **bottom third**. Major and minor fifth chords are the most commonly used chords in music.

The **major fifth chord** consists of a **major third** and a **perfect fifth**.
- It is built on a major third, giving it a **major quality**.

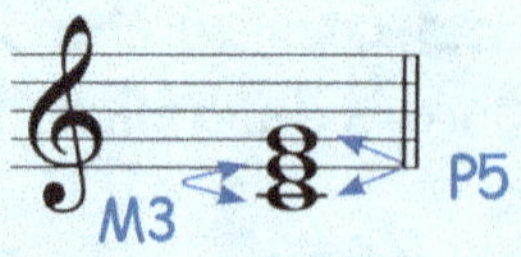

The **minor fifth chord** consists of a **minor third** and a **perfect fifth**.
- It is built on a **minor third**, giving it a **minor quality**.

INVERSIONS

- the **root position** = a **fifth chord** (5)
- the **1ˢᵗ inversion** = a **sixth chord** (6)
  - is created by moving the root note of a fifth chord an octave higher
- the **2ⁿᵈ inversion** = a **four-six chord** (6/4)
  - is created by moving the bottom note of a six chord an octave higher

Examples from the note C:

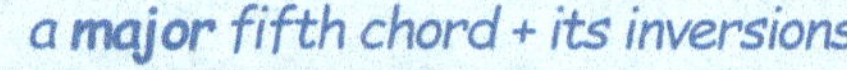
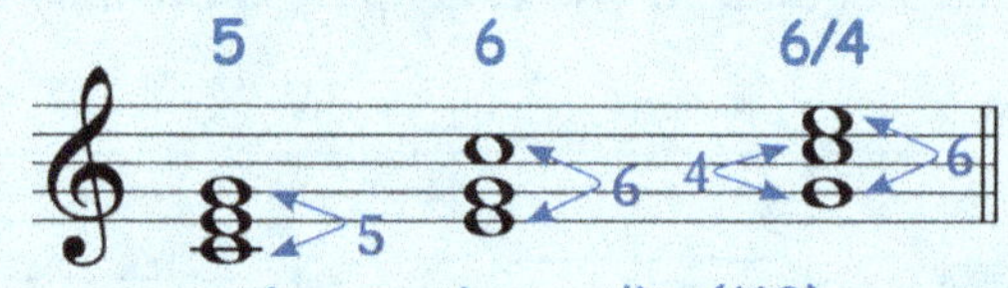

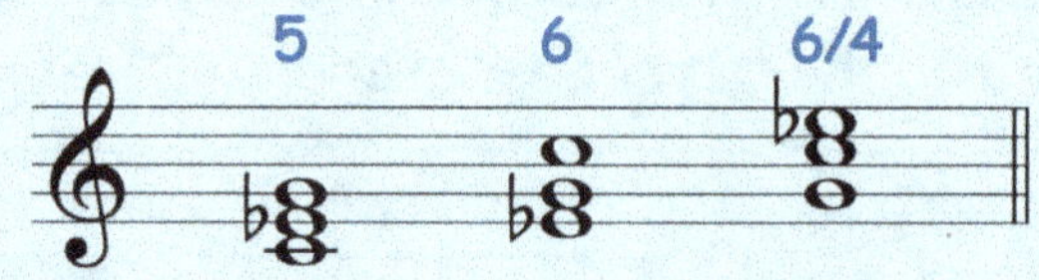

E Notate major and minor fifth chords from the assigned notes. Label the major chords as "M" and the minor ones as "m."

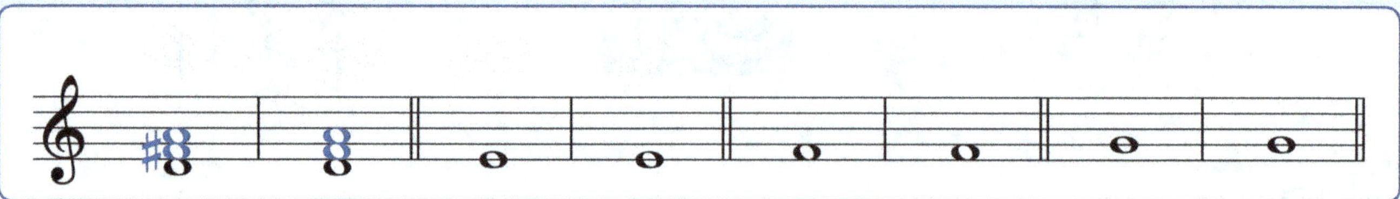

E Write the number indicating the root position or inversions (5, 6, 6/4) of the chords into the boxes below each chord. Circle all major chords.

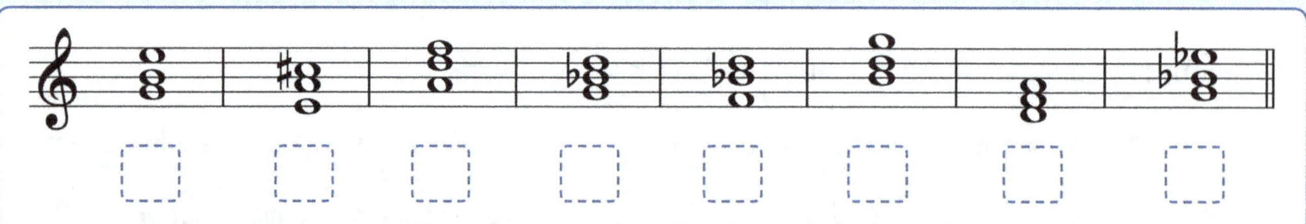

DIMINISHED & AUGMENTED FIFTH CHORD

ROOT POSITIONS

The **diminished fifth chord** = a minor third and a **diminished fifth**.
- It's derived from a minor fifth chord by diminishing the upper third from major to minor = **two stacked minor thirds**.

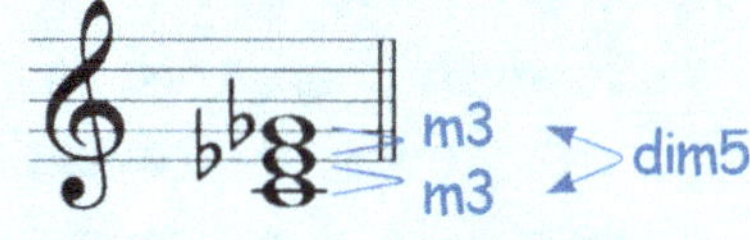

The **augmented fifth chord** = a major third and an **augmented fifth**.
- It's derived from the major chord by augmenting the upper third from minor to major = **two stacked major thirds**.

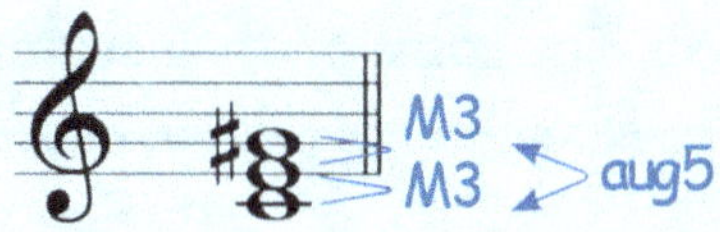

INVERSIONS

The fifth chord has two inversions: the **sixth chord** and the **four-sixth chord**. This same principle applies to the inversions of both diminished and augmented fifth chords. To clarify the quality of these inversions, we add their respective extensions: either a **diminished** or **augmented sixth** or a **four-sixth chord**.

Examples from the note C:

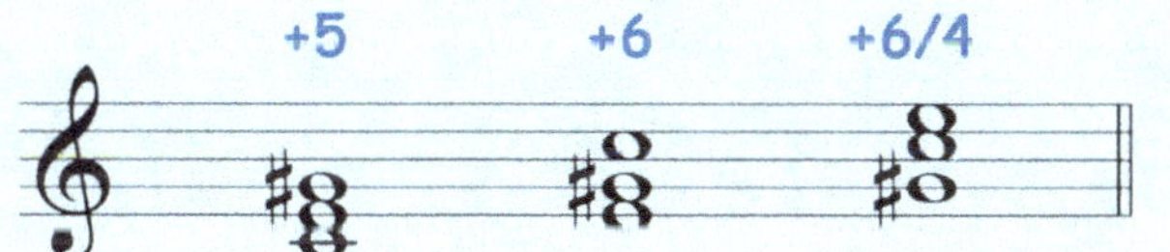

E Draw blue brackets to indicate diminished fifths and green brackets to indicate augmented fifths. Circle all diminished fifth chords.

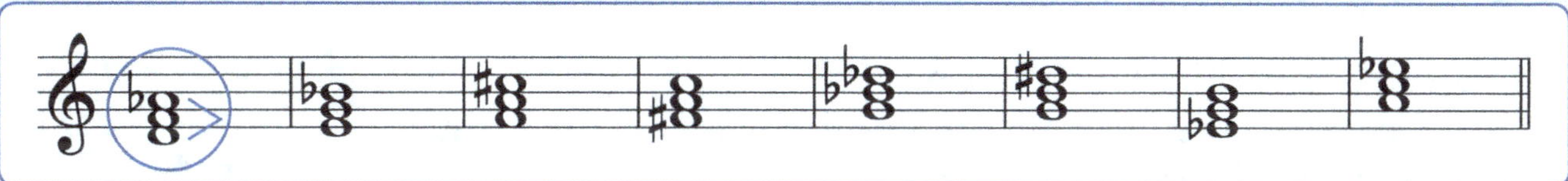

E Link the boxes containing the fifth chord and both its inversions (see the example). Color the box with the diminished fifth chord.

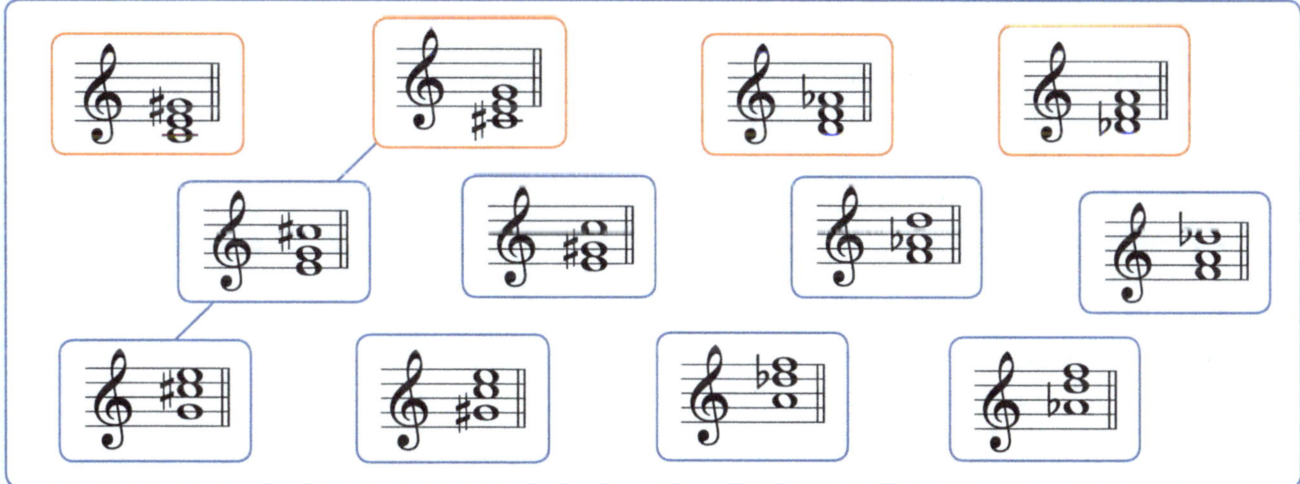

SEVENTH CHORDS

- **Seventh chords** are **four-note chords**. Their characteristic interval (the distance between the two outer tones) is **a seventh (7)**.
- A seventh chord consist of a **fifth chord** and a **seventh** = three stacked thirds.
- The **name** of the seventh chord signifies the **quality** of the **fifth chord** and of the **seventh**.
  Example: the major/major seventh chord will have the major fifth chord and the major seventh.

By altering the fifth chord and the seventh, we can create up to **seven basic seventh chords**.
Four of them are commonly used:
- **dominant seventh chord (D7)** = a major fifth chord and a minor seventh
- **major seventh chord** = a major fifth chord and a major seventh
- **minor seventh chord** = a minor fifth chord and a minor seventh
- **diminished seventh chord** = a diminished fifth chord and a diminished seventh

DOMINANT SEVENTH CHORD - D7

- the major fifth chord + the minor seventh
- it's called "dominant" because its root position is built on the dominant = the 5th degree of a scale
- the most utilized seventh chord

NINTH CHORD

- the **ninth chord** is a **five-note chord**
- its characteristic interval is the **ninth (9)** - (the distance between the two outer tones)
- it consists of the **seventh chord** and a **ninth** = four stacked thirds

Dominant Ninth Chord - D9

- **major D9** = the dominant seventh chord + a major ninth
- **minor D9** = the dominant seventh chord + a minor ninth

BASIC TYPES OF CHORDS OVERVIEW

FIFTH CHORDS

Fifth chords' (5) root positions (built from the note C4):

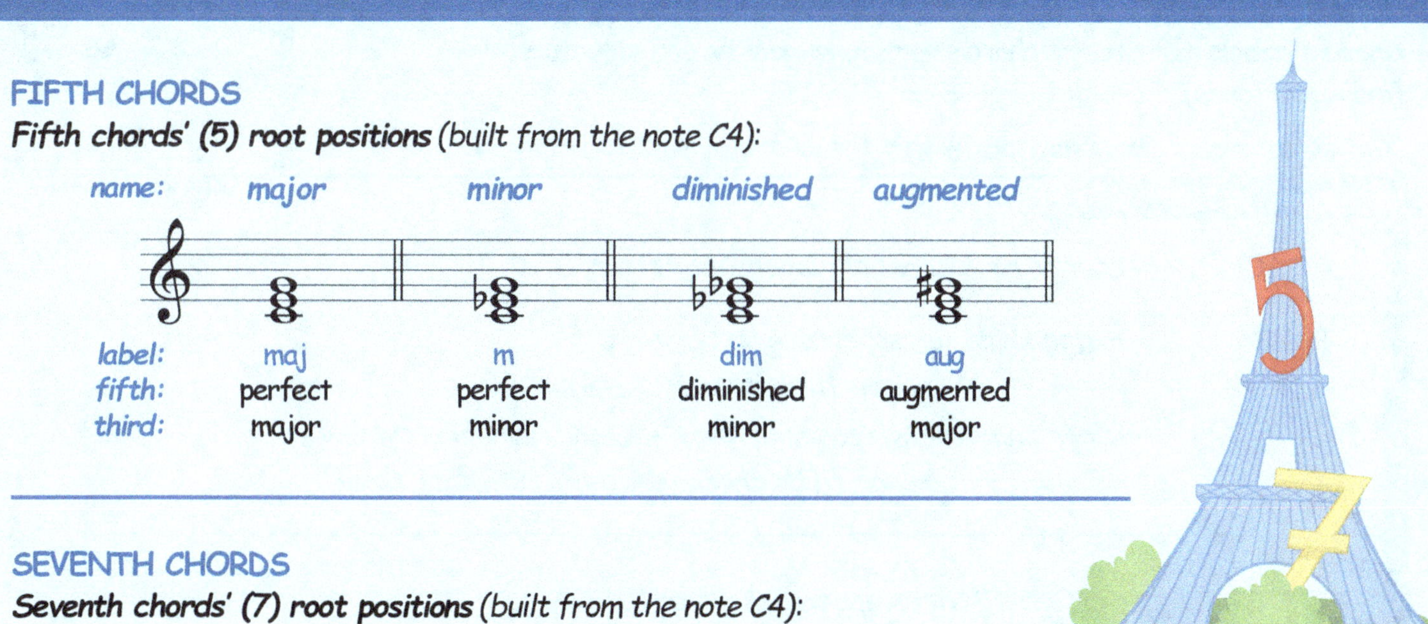

SEVENTH CHORDS

Seventh chords' (7) root positions (built from the note C4):

Short quality names of the fourth most commonly used seventh chords:

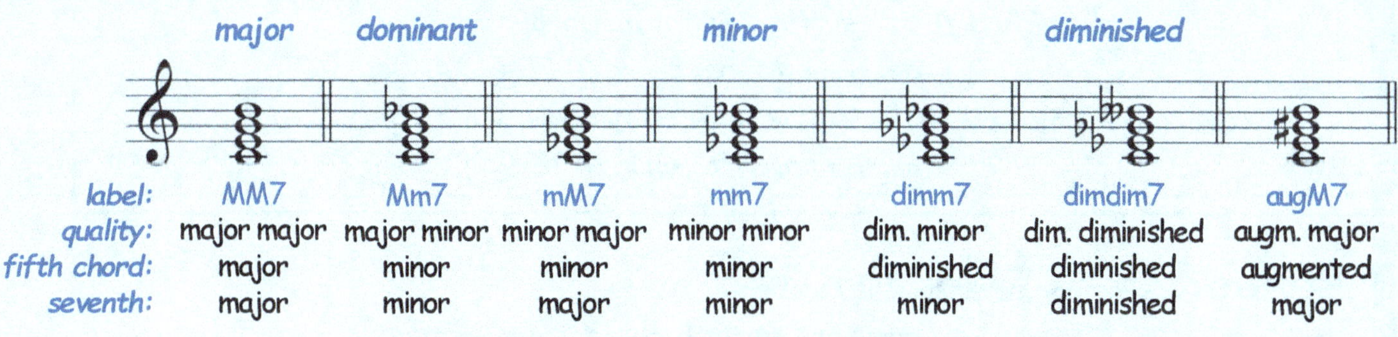

E Use a green bracket to indicate major fifth chords and a blue bracket to indicate minor fifth chords. Correctly label each seventh chord using one of the following labels: Mm, MM, or mm.

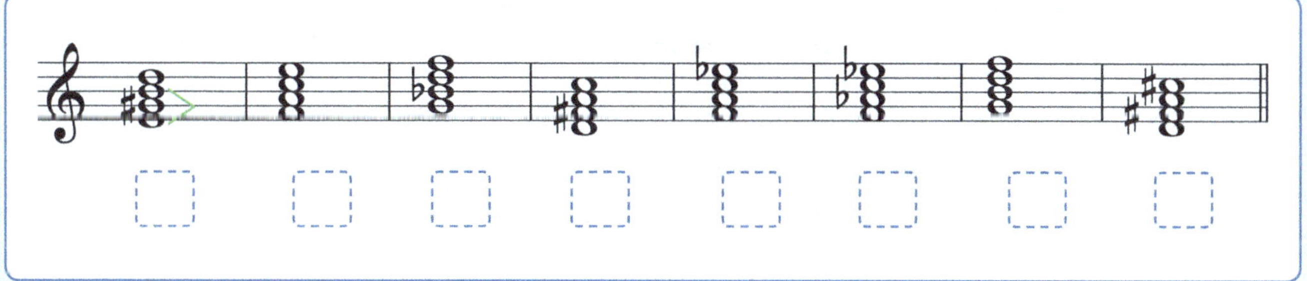

E Notate the dominant seventh chord (Mm7) from the assigned notes. Remember the D7 structure - a major fifth chord and a minor seventh.

CHORD SYMBOLS

Chord symbols are **abbreviated indicators for chords**, typically placed above the melody. They serve as guides for **harmonic accompaniment**.

Chord symbols indicate the chord's **root tone**, **quality**, and **structure** (individual tones).

The structure of the indicators within the chord symbol is firmly set.

Examples from the tone C:

UNISON — chord's **root tone**: an **uppercase letter**, i.e. **C**

THIRD — **major third**: an uppercase letter, i.e. **C**
    major fifth chord (C-E-G) = C
— **minor third**: +lowercase suffixes: **-m**, **-mi**, **-min**, or a symbol: **–**
    minor fifth chord (C-Eb-G) = Cm, Cmi, Cmin, C–

FIFTH

— **perfect fifth**: an uppercase letter, i.e. **C**
    major fifth chord (C-E-G) = C
— **diminished fifth**: +suffix: **-dim**, or a symbols: **°**
    diminished fifth chord (C-Eb-Gb) = Cdim , C°
— **augmented fifth**: +suffix: **-aug**, or symbols: **+**, **+5**, **$\sharp$5**
    augmented fifth chord (C-E-G#) = Caug, C+, C^{+5}, $C^{\sharp 5}$

SEVENTH
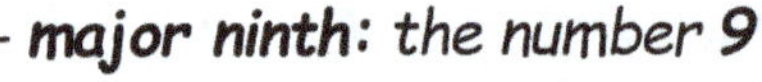
— **minor seventh**: the number **7**
    dominant seventh chord (C-E-G-Bb) = C^{7}
    minor seventh chord (C-Eb-G-Bb) = Cm^{7}
— **major seventh**: +suffixes: **-maj**^{7}, **M**^{7}
    major seventh chord (C-E-G-B) = $Cmaj^{7}$, CM^{7}
— **diminished seventh**: +suffix: **-dim**, or a symbol: **°**
    diminished seventh chord (C-Eb-Gb-Bbb) = $Cdim^{7}$, $C°^{7}$

NINTH

— **major ninth**: the number **9**
    dominant ninth chord (C-E-G-Bb-D) = C^{9}

ADDED TONE

*If we decide to **add a note** to a chord, we **mark it** by the **number** indicating its degree within the scale.*

added sixth: the number **6**

fifth chords with added sixth: (C-E-G-A) = C^{6} , (C-Eb-G-A) = Cm^{6}

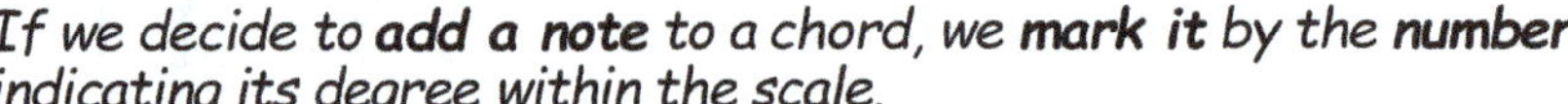

COMMONLY USED CHORDS

Examples from the tone C:

fifth chords

major fifth chord	minor fifth chord	diminished fifth chord	augmented fifth chord
C	Cm, Cmi	Cdim, C°	Caug, C+

seventh chords

dominant seventh chord	major seventh chord	minor seventh chord	diminished seventh chord
C^7	$Cmaj^7$, CM^7	Cm^7	$Cdim^7$, $C°^7$

ninth chord

dominant ninth chord C^9

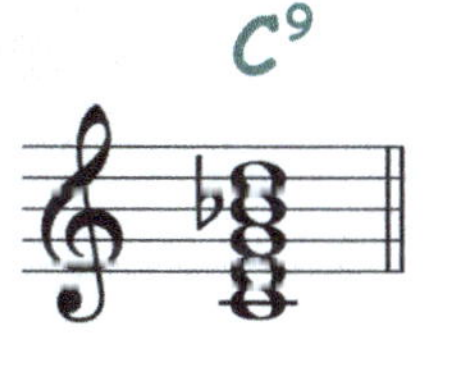

added tone

major fifth chord with added sixth C^6

H

B

The **diagram** contains the chords in their **root positions** only. Each chord can be used in all of its inversions. The **chord inversions** and their chord symbols are described in the following chapter.

The chord symbols may vary slightly from country to country. The most notable difference is when indicating the note B.

1. The European names: the primary tone - H; altered notes - B (b) or His (#).
2. The American names: the primary tone - B; altered notes - Bb and B#.

CHORD INVERSIONS

FIFTH CHORD INVERSIONS

The fifth chord inversions are the sixth and four-sixth chords.

- the **root position** = a **fifth chord (5)**
- the **1st inversion** = a **sixth chord (6)** is created by moving the root note an octave higher.
- the **2nd inversion** = a **four-sixth chord (6/4)** is created by moving the sixth chord's bottom note an octave higher.

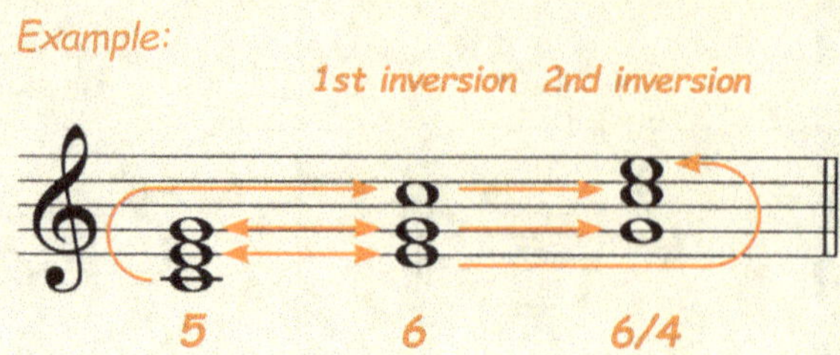

SEVENTH CHORD INVERSIONS

The **seventh chord inversions** are the first inversion - a 5/6 chord, the second inversion - a 4/3 chord, and the fourth inversion - a 4/2 chord. Those inversions apply to all types of seventh chords.

The **inversions' numeric symbols** contain the **inversion's characteristic interval(s)**: 5/6 - a fifth chord plus a sixth, 4/3 - a third and a fourth in the core of the chord, 4/2 - a second between the two low notes and the fourth in the core of the chord.

The most common seventh chord is the **dominant seventh** chord and its inversions.

- the **root position** = a **seventh** chord **(7)**
- the **1st inversion** = a **five-six** chord **(6/5)**
  - it's created by moving the root note an octave higher.
- the **2nd inversion** = a **three-four** chord **(4/3)**
  - it's created by moving the first inversion's bottom note an octave higher.
- the **3rd inversion** = a **two-four** chord **(4/2 or 2)**
  - it's created by moving the second inversion's bottom note an octave higher.

Inversions of the C seventh chord - C7:

E Notate the inversions of the chords on the staff.

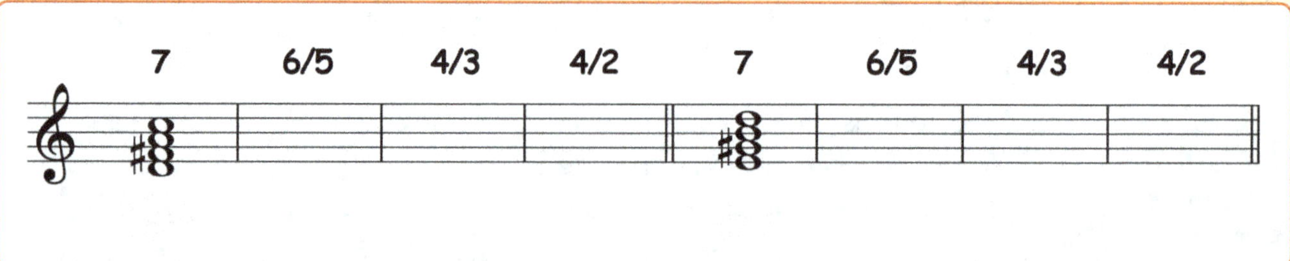

CHORD INVERSION CHORD SYMBOLS

The chord inversion label contains **two stacked pieces of information** separated by the divider.

1. the **chord** symbol in its **root position**

2. the **bottom tone** of the **inversion**

Example:

$$\frac{\textbf{Cm}}{\textbf{Eb}}$$

Cm = C minor fifth chord
Eb = 1ˢᵗ inversion (Eb-G-C)
Eb at the bottom

$$\frac{\textbf{C}^7}{\textbf{G}}$$

C⁷ = dominnat seventh chord
G = 2ⁿᵈ inversion (G-Bb-C-E)
G at the bottom

E Notate the fifth chords and their inversions according to the chord labels below the staff.

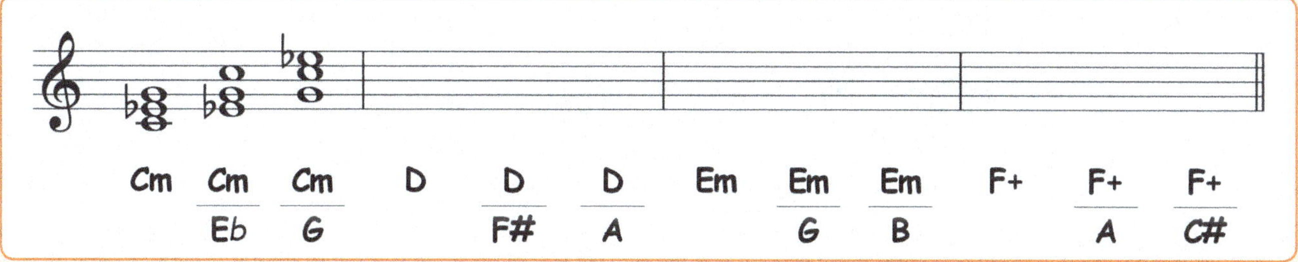

E Link the chords with their correct symbols.

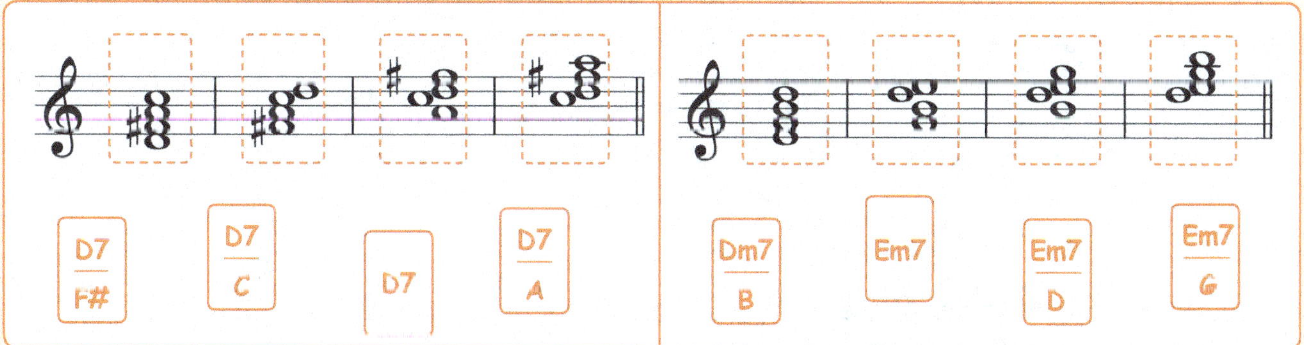

Chord Symbols With the Divider
The part of the symbol located below the divider represents the bass note of the chord. We use this type of chord symbol for all chords where the lowest note differs from the lowest note of the chord in its root position.

Fifth Chords

E Notate major, minor, diminished, and augmented fifth chords from the assigned tones.

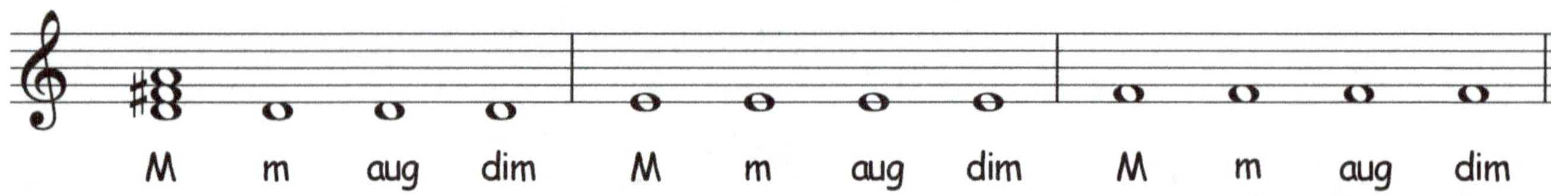

Fifth Chord's Inversions

E Notate the inversions of the assigned fifth chords

E Link the belonging boxes.

Seventh Chords

E Built dominant, major, and minor seventh chords from the assigned root notes. Use blue brackets to mark the minor seventh and the green ones to mark the major seventh.

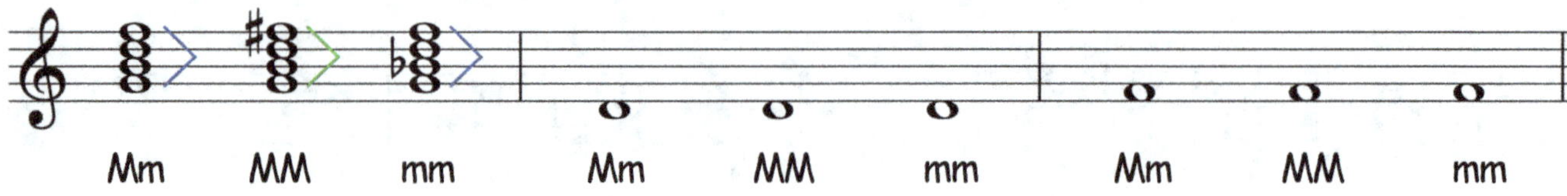

Dominant Seventh Chord Inversions

E 1. Notate the inversions of the assigned dominant seventh chord

C^7

2. Name all the inversions with their full name

7 - *root position: the seventh chord*

6/5 -

4/3 -

4/2 -

Chord Labels - Fifth Chords and Their Inversions

E Write the correct chord symbols into the boxes above and below the assigned chords.

E Circle the correctly labeled examples.

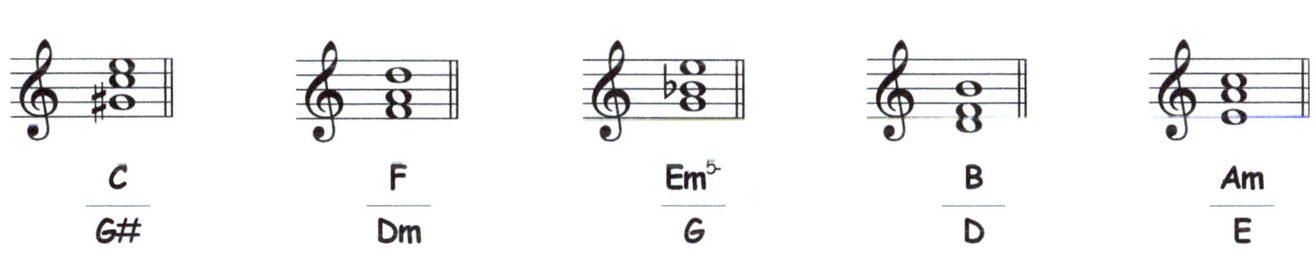

Chord Symbols - Seventh Chords and Their Inversions

E Link the belonging boxes.

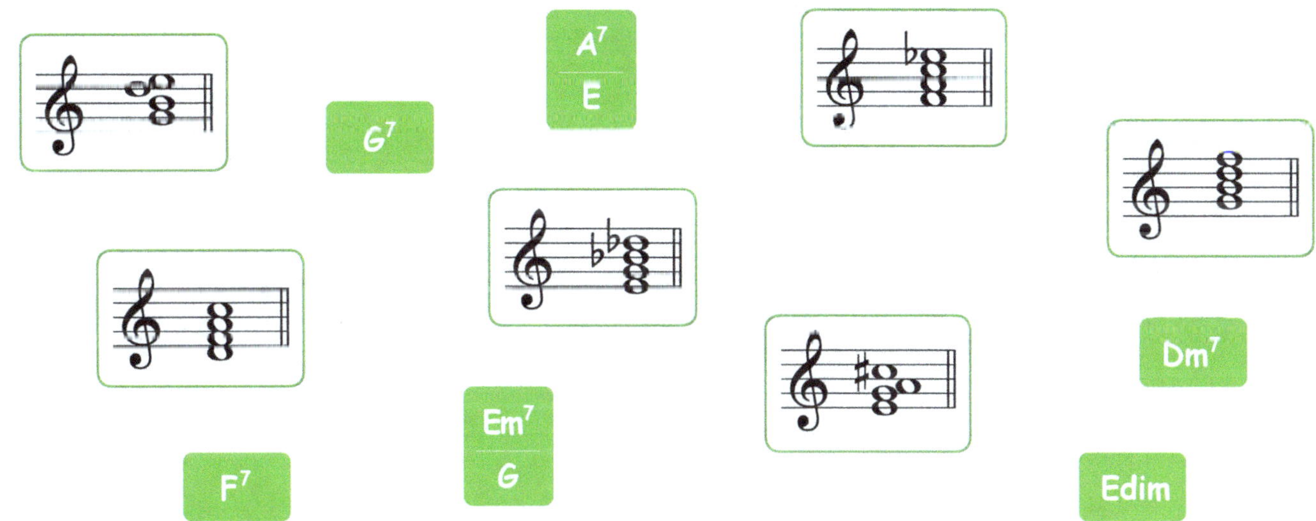

FUNDAMENTALS OF HARMONY

HARMONY

Harmony is the area of music theory about **constructing and connecting chords**. The term "harmony" originates from the ancient Greek word "harmonia," which means "a joint, an agreement, or concord." In music, to "**harmonize**" refers to creating tone clusters made up of two or more tones. There are rules that govern how to properly harmonize **individual tones**, meaning **connecting them correctly and effectively**.

SCALE DEGREES

- To **describe scale degrees**, we use either numbers or names, each representing its meaning and function. The fundamental scale degrees are the 1st, 4th, and 5th degrees.
- **Harmonic functions** are chords built on these **scale degrees**, and all chords must utilize the notes contained within their scale.
- The **fundamental harmonic functions** are built on the fundamental scale degrees.
  Their names are: **T**onic = the **1st degree**, **S**ubdominant = the **4th degree**, **D**ominant = the 5th degree. These three chords contain **all the notes of their scale**.

HARMONIC FUNCTIONS OF MAJOR SCALE
Major Scale Degrees

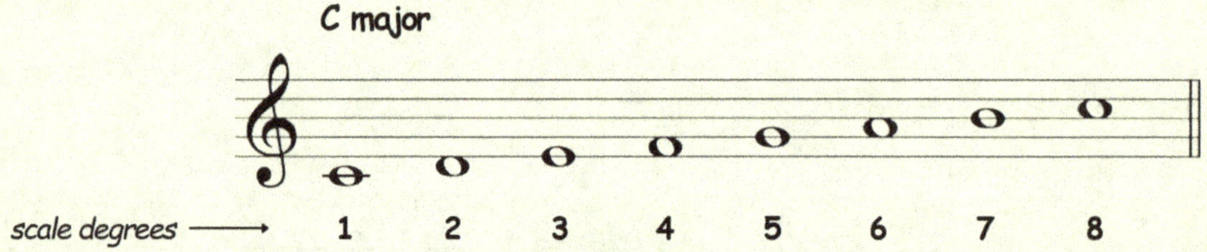

Fifth Chords Built on Major Scale Degrees

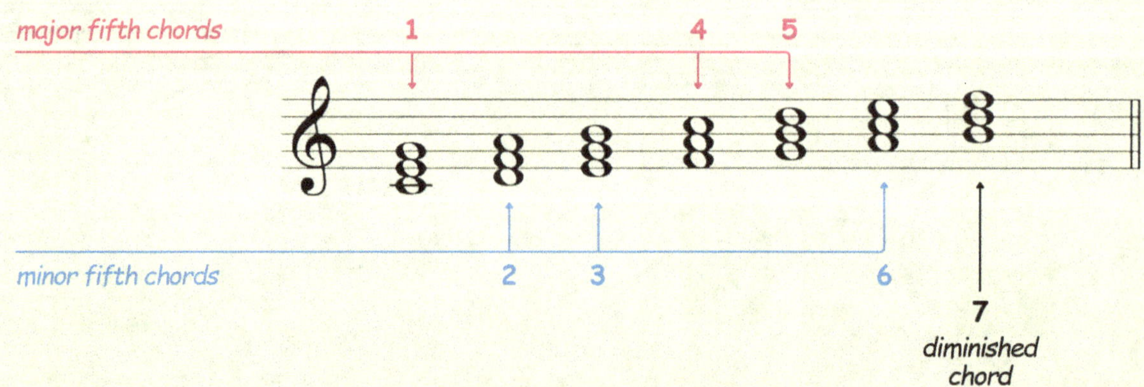

HARMONIC FUNCTIONS OF MINOR SCALES
Minor Scale Degrees

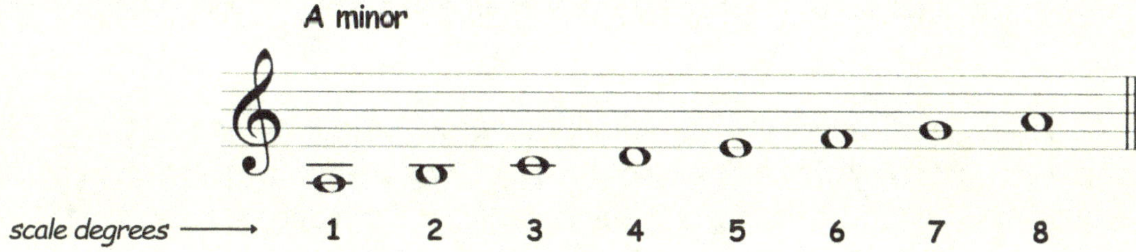

Fifth Chords Built on Minor Scale Degrees

The A natural minor scale:

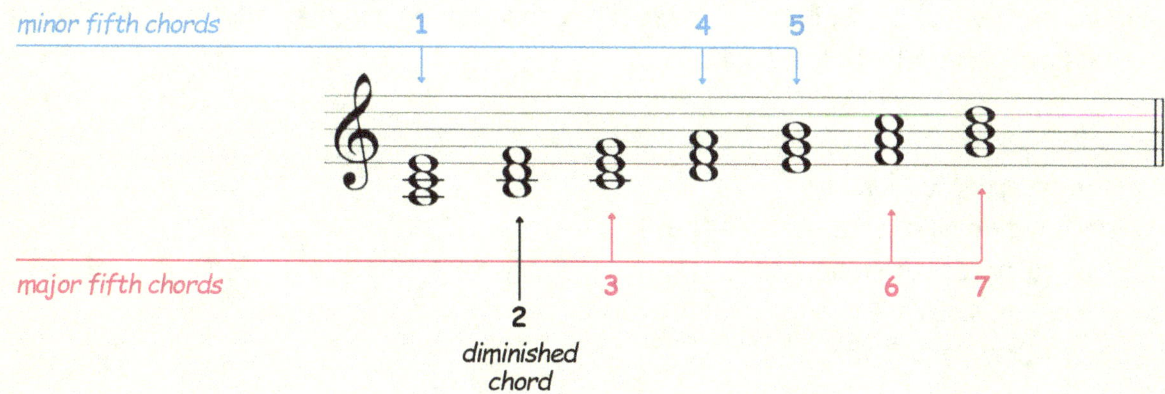

The natural (Aeolian) scale is the original minor scale with unique harmonizing qualities. Over time, it evolved to align with the major scale, leading to the creation of two new minor scales: the **melodic** and **harmonic** minor scales. These scales have both minor and **major** chords on their fundamental degrees.

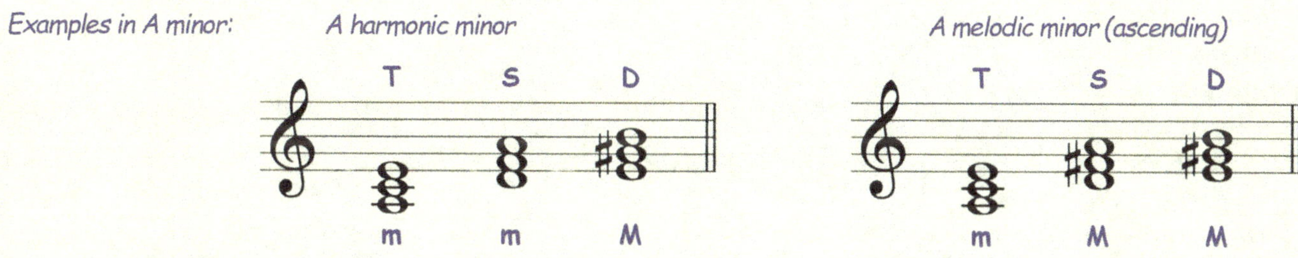

E   Notate fifth chords in the keys of F major, D major and D minor at the assigned degrees. Circle the major chords (M3).

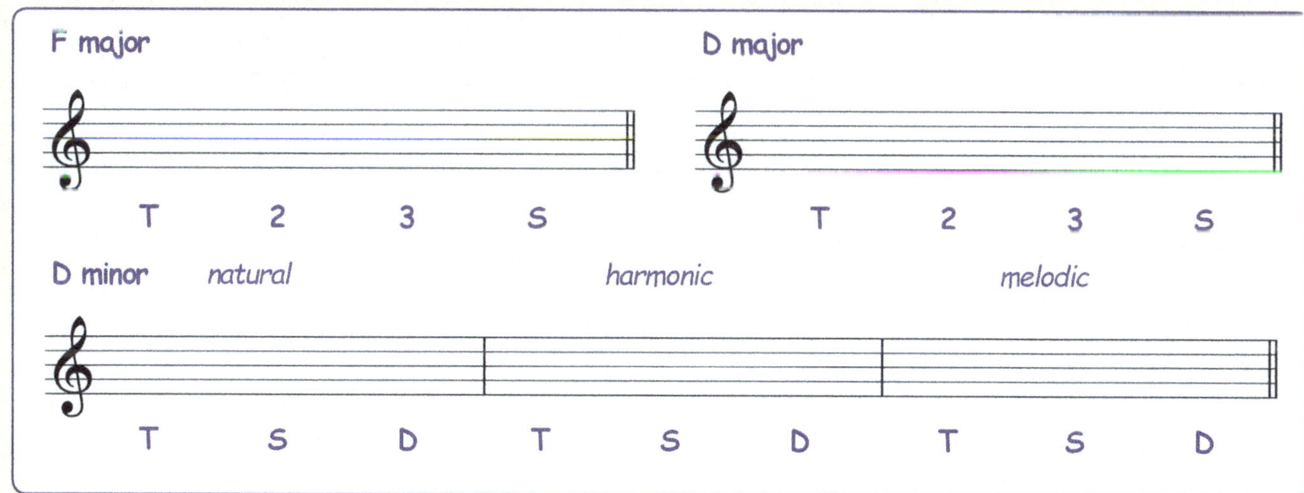

FUNCTIONALITY OF INDIVIDUAL HARMONIC FUNCTIONS

Harmony is essentially built on triad - fifth chords built on all seven degrees of a diatonic scale. We call them harmonic functions. These harmonic functions are divided into two groups: fundamental and additional (secondary).

Fundamental harmonic functions are chords built on the fundamental scale degrees. Together, they are so functional and powerful that any of the folk songs can be accompanied using just those. Fundamental harmonic functions are: 1st degree = Tonic, 4th degree = Subdominant, and 5th degree = Dominant.

Additional or secondary harmonic functions are chords built on the remaining scale degrees. We use them for the harmonization of more complex melodies and harmonic enrichment. Scale degrees on which the additional harmonic functions are built also have names. Still, we refer to the chords built on them and their harmonic functions mostly just by number: **2nd degree** - *Supertonic*, **3rd degree** - *Mediant*, **6th degree** - *Submediant*, **7th degree** - *Leading Tone or Subtonic*.

MAJOR KEY CADENCE

Cadence refers to the progression of fundamental chords within a key that leads to the conclusion of a musical phrase or composition. The simplest cadence progression is:
Tonic-Subdominant-Dominant-Tonic.

Connecting Chords - Chord Progression

*Chord **inversions** are best for creating smooth connections between chords - chord progression. Using so-called **voice leading**, we lead each voice the **shortest possible way** from the tone of one chord to the next one. Tones that are part of both neighboring chords may be connected using a tie. Other voices move to the closest possible tone contained in the target chord.*

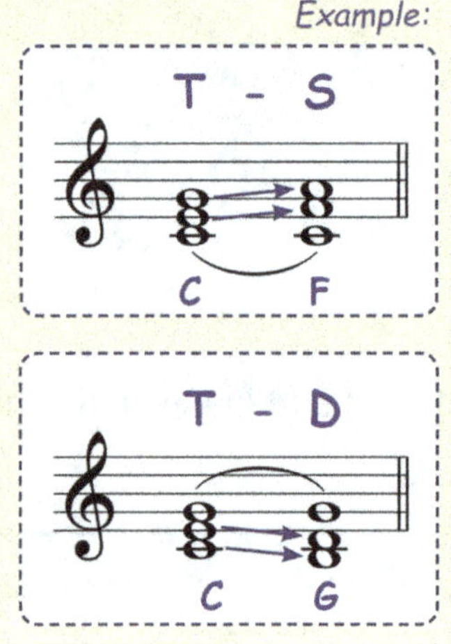

E   Find the most direct way to connect the assigned harmonic functions in the keys of G and F major.

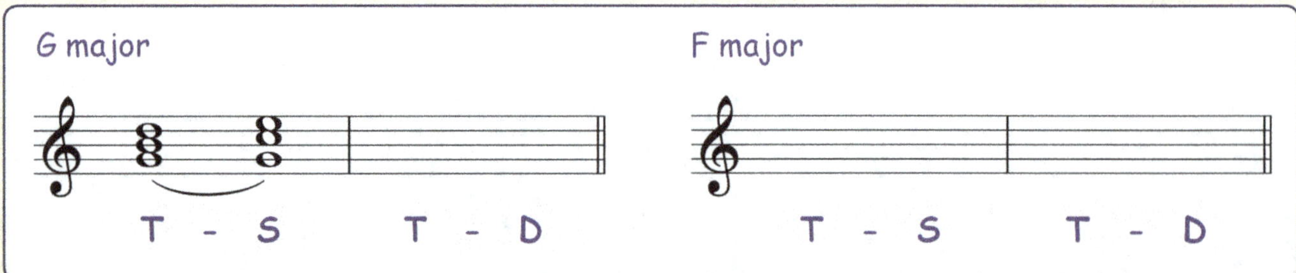

How do we choose which tone to use for harmonization?
Selecting chords depends on the tones of a melody. *Let's learn how to align chords with individual tones of a melodic line. At first, we will use only fifth chords.*

A fifth chord is a triad. We can use it for the harmonization of three individual tones.

Example:
C major fifth chord (C-E-G) can be used to accompany tones C, E, and G

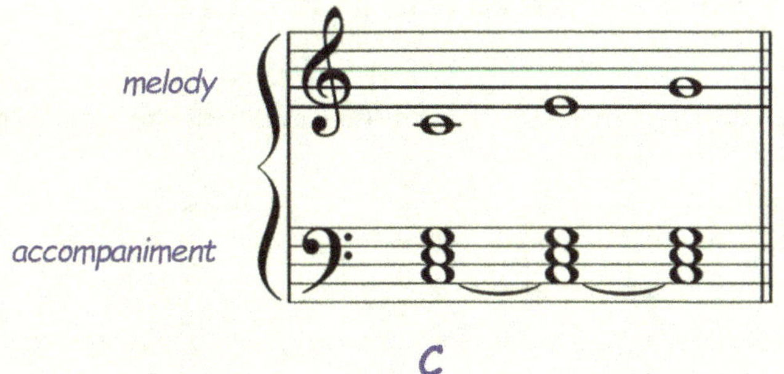

One melodic tone can be part of several fifth chords

Example:
The tone C is part of fifth chords:
C (C_E_G), F (F-A-C), Am (A-C-E)…

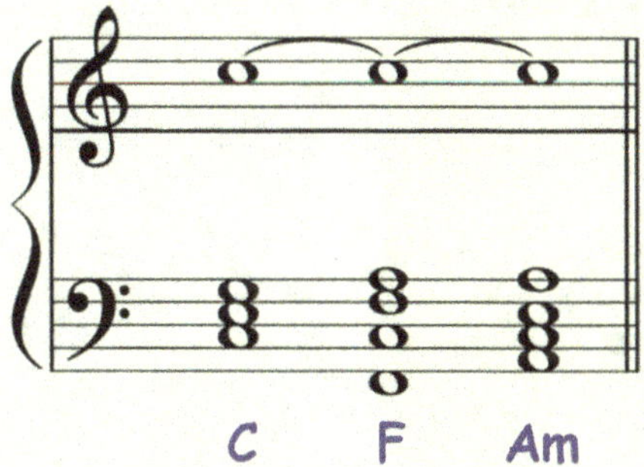

E Notate a fifth chord suitable for accompanying the assigned notes in every measure.

E What common tone do all three chords share? Write it in the boxes above each measure.

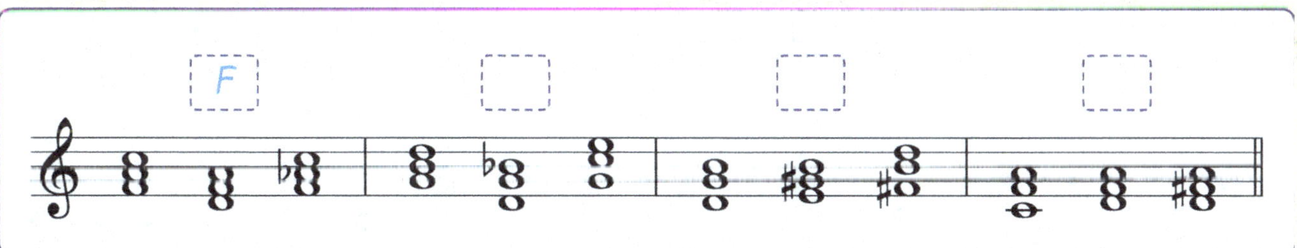

*Every melody can be harmonized in several ways. Within the given rules, we can choose many different chords to accompany a single melody. Various musical styles, genres, and cultures use unique methods for harmonizing melodies. People with a **sense for harmonizing** have the talent to harmonize melodies effortlessly.*

MELODY HARMONIZATION

When harmonizing a melody, it is essential to identify the **key harmonic (anchor) tones** and **melodic tones**. The anchor tones primarily occur on the strong beats, while the melodic tones contribute richness and complexity to the melodic line.

Melodic tones are the **individual notes within a melody** that **do not** necessarily **align with the harmony**. When a melody is played alongside harmonic accompaniment, the notes in the melody change more frequently than the notes in the harmonic accompaniment. This means that a single chord can support multiple melodic tones. Tones that do not belong to the harmony (the accompanying chord) are referred to as melodic tones.

Clefi & Notelina's Songbook, pg. 50
When I Passed the City Gate

Accompanying Songs Using Chord Symbols

in songbooks, chord labels above the melody typically indicate the accompaniment, as you can see in Clefi's Songbooks.

Hints for Successful Accompaniment

- The chord indicated by a chord label **remains valid** until a new chord is specified.
- The **accompaniment is based** on the **root tone** of the **indicated chord**. Therefore, it's advisable to begin by accompanying the melody using only the bass tone represented by the letter of the chord label.
- Once comfortable with the root tone, you can start to **incorporate the middle tones** (voices).
- Initially, it's beneficial to play the accompanying chord only on the heavy beats.

Example of a simple accompaniment:

Clefi & Notelina's Songbook, pg. 50
When I Passed the City Gate

Harmonic Rhythm of Accompaniment

While harmonizing and creating an accompaniment, we must decide on **harmonic rhythm.**
Chords should amplify the impact of accented beats and, as such, be part of the harmonic rhythm.

In **simple measures**, we can play:
- a whole chord on the downbeat
- the bass tone on the downbeat and the chord's middle voices on the soft beat (on the second beat in 2/4 measure, on the second and third beats in 3/4 measure)

Accompaniment examples:

In **combined measures**, we apply the harmonic rhythmic pattern from simple measures. For example, in a 4/4 measure, we can use a consecutive 2/4 harmonic rhythmic pattern, placing more emphasis on the downbeat than on the third beat.

E Create a simple accompaniment. See the first measure for inspiration.

Clefi & Notelina's Songbook, pg. 57
Our Little Castle

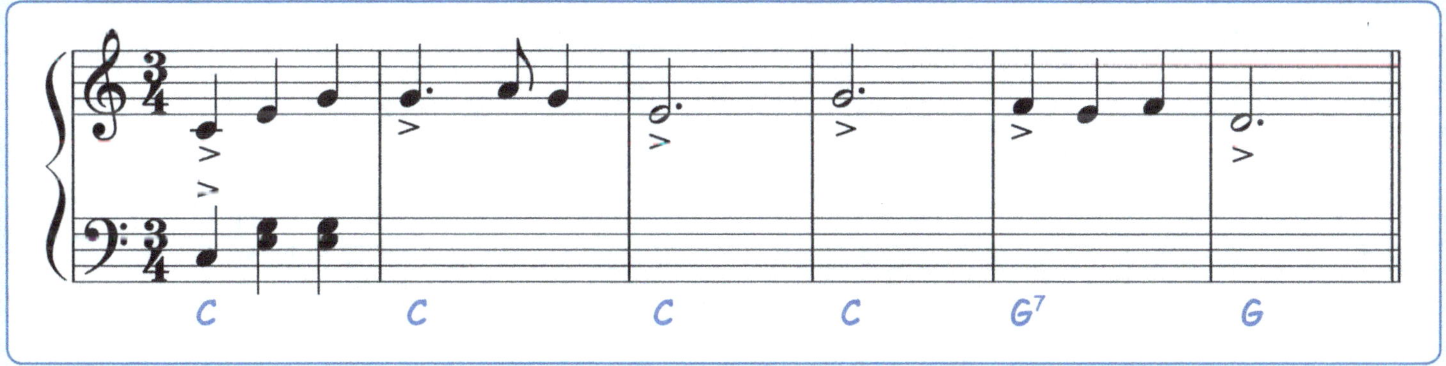

Every musical instrument provides unique ways for creating accompaniment.
When collaborating with other musicians, everyone needs to work together in maintaining a consistent
harmonic progression and rhythm.

MUSICAL TERMS IN HARMONY

TRANSPOSITION AND MODULATION

- **Transposition** is process of **moving of a composition from one key to another.**

Example of transposition from C major to G major:

Bedřich Smetana - *"Why Shouldn't We Rejoice"*
from *"The Bartered Bride."*

- **Modulation** is a **transition from one key to another within a composition** via modulating tones and chords.

Example of modulation from G major to Ab major:

Bedřich Smetana - *"The Moldau"*

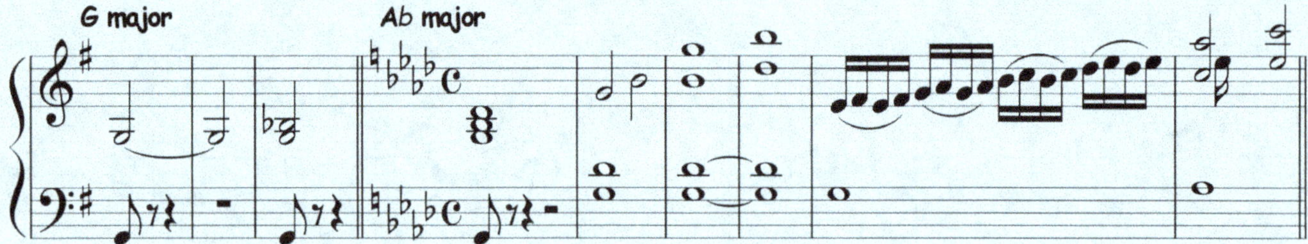

CONSONANCE AND DISSONANCE

- **Consonance**: a pleasing sound, agreeable and comforting harmony.
- **Dissonance**: an unpleasant sound marked by aggravating disharmony.

A **cluster of tones**, whether intervals or chords, can be classified as either **consonant** or **dissonant**, depending on its structure and the intervals used. The acceptance of these sound clusters has evolved throughout history; some combinations that are commonly accepted today were once considered unacceptable. Additionally, the perception of sounds and their combinations varies from culture to culture.

HOMOPHONY AND POLYPHONY

- Homophony: a single voice (melody) with an accompaniment
- Polyphony: multiple voices (melodies) sang or played simultaneously

Example of homophony:

Example of polyphony:

W. A. Mozart - *"Sonate in C major"*

J.S. Bach - *"Invention"*

EXERCISES

Cadence and Transposition

E Tranpose the C major cadence into assigned keys. Use either key signatures or free standing accidentals

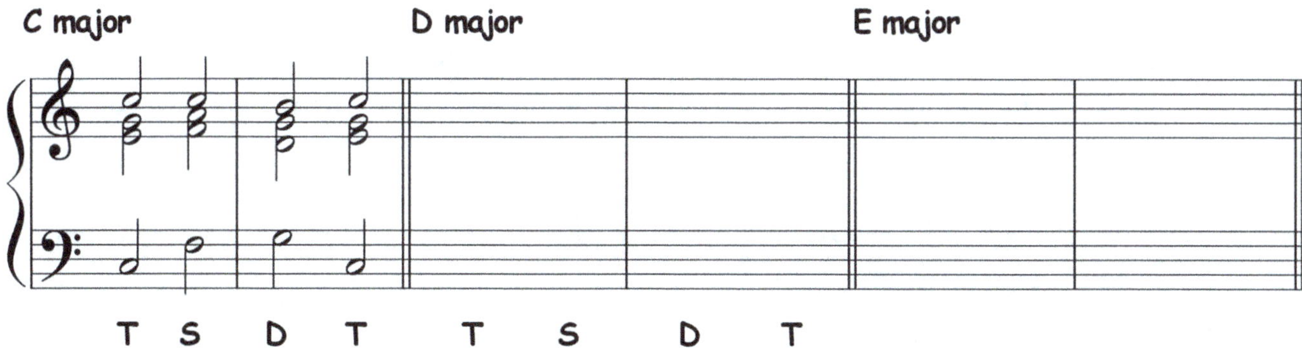

Chord Progression

E Progress from the fifth chords or inversions with other fundamental harmonic functions the shortest possible way.

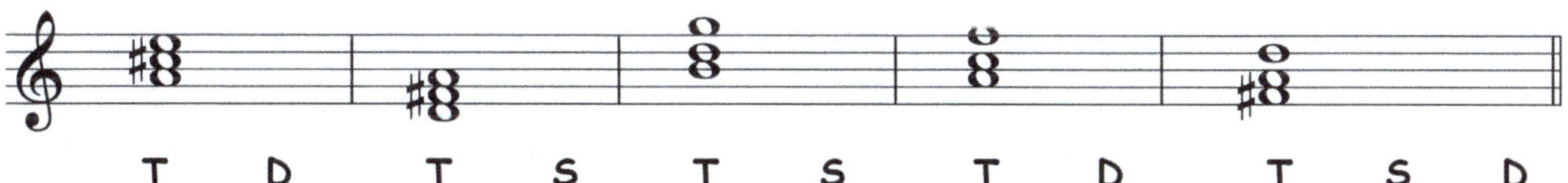

E Link the chord label to most suitable melodic tones.

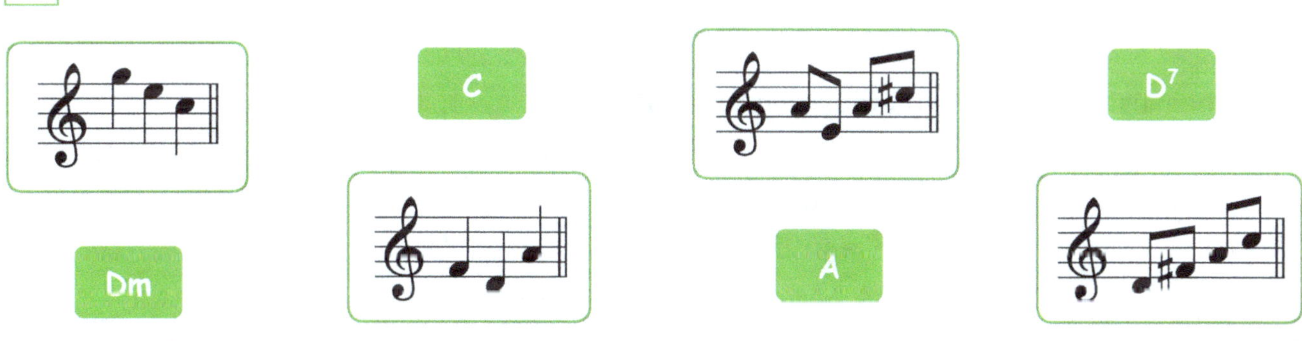

Musical Terms

E Describe the meaning of the following musical terms:

homophony: ....

polyphony: ....

consonance: ....

dissonance: ....

MUSIC TERMINOLOGY

Music terminology refers to the set of names and terms used in music and musical notation. These terms help clarify how to sing or play compositions. Most of these terms are derived from Italian.

Music terminology can be categorized into four general groups:

- **dynamics** – markings, terms and signs indicating **volume** and its **modifications**
- **tempo** – markings, terms and signs indicating **speed** and **its modifications**
- **expression** – markings, terms, and signs indicating performance **feelings, manner,** and **directions**
- **articulations** – markings, terms, and signs indicating **character**, **style**, and **clarity** of **tones** and **performance**

Altering a Music Sign or Term

If we need to alter dynamics, tempo, or expression in the middle of a piece, we use music terms to express our intention to adjust tempo or expression.

Here are a few examples:

- meno - less
- più - more
- poco - a bit
- molto - very, much
- subito - suddenly

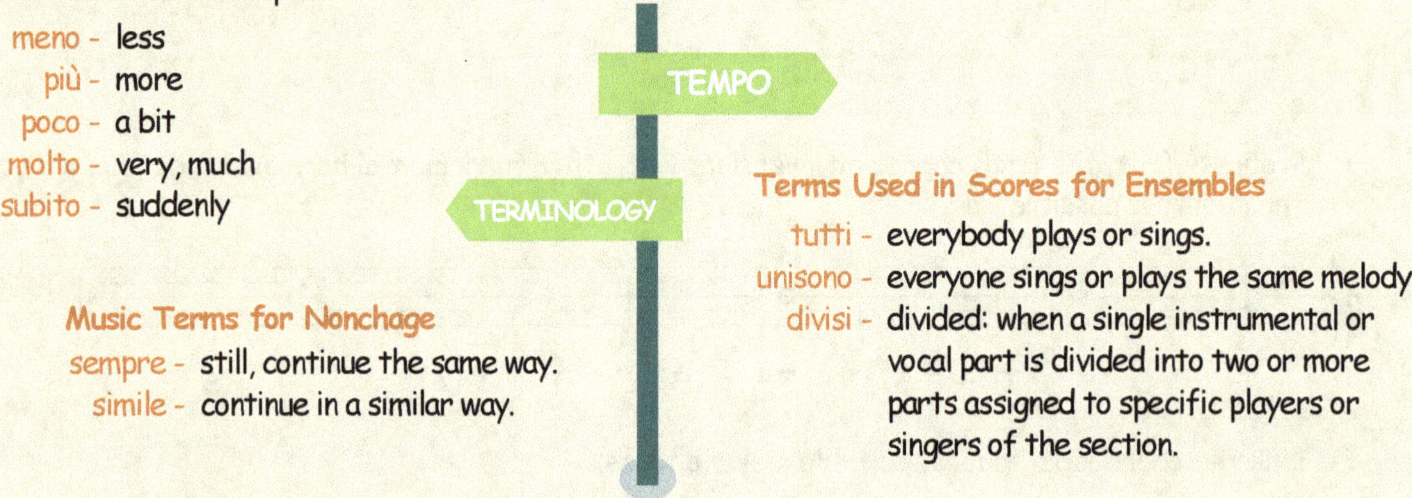

Terms Used in Scores for Ensembles

- tutti - everybody plays or sings.
- unisono - everyone sings or plays the same melody.
- divisi - divided: when a single instrumental or vocal part is divided into two or more parts assigned to specific players or singers of the section.

Music Terms for Nonchage

- sempre - still, continue the same way.
- simile - continue in a similar way.

E Link the music terms with their appropriate categories.

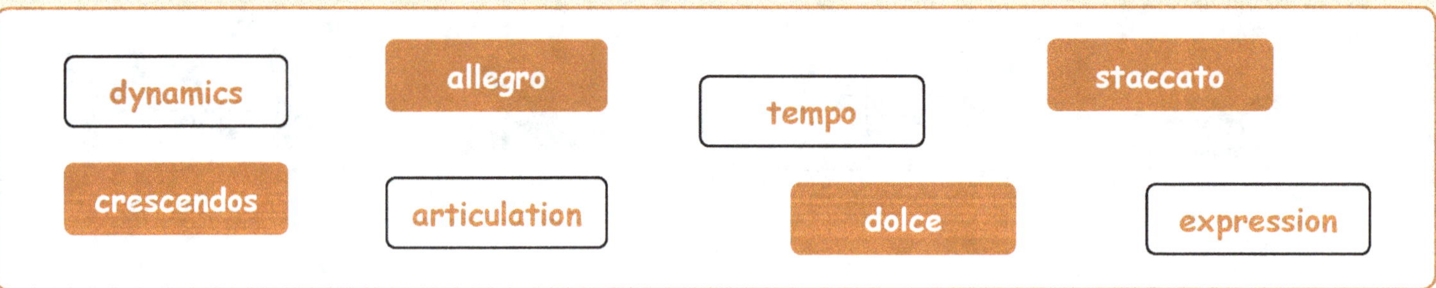

E On the line below, line up the following tempo markings from the fastest to the slowest:
andante, largo, presto, allegro, moderato, adagio.

TEMPO

Tempo refers to the speed of a regular rhythm or movement.

It can be indicated using either a musical term or a numerical value that expresses the number of beats per minute. A device used to measure the exact tempo is called a **metronome**.

Metronomes feature a scale that displays various tempo markings. By selecting a specific marking, we can determine the speed of the beats and their frequency per minute or beats per minute - **BPM**.

Tempo Markings

In the following table, we see the most common tempo markings, their meanings, and tempo values.

tempo marking	meaning	BPM
grave	heavy	40
largo	broad	44
lento	lengthily	50
adagio	slow	54
largetto	somewhat broadly	60
andante	walking pace	63
andantino	faster walking pace	69
sostenuto	calm and steady	76
commodo	comfortably	84
maestoso	majestically, with dignity	88
moderato	moderately	94
allegretto	somewhat quickly	104
allegro moderato	moderately fast	120
allegro	happily (fast)	132
allegro assai	very fast (and happily)	144
vivace	lively fast	160
presto	briskly fast	182
prestissimo	as fast as possible	208

Direct Tempo Changes

poco meno - a bit slower, calmer

meno mosso - less moving, slower

più mosso - with more movement, faster

animato - livelier

tempo I - in original tempo

Gradual Tempo Changes

accelerando - gradually faster

ritardanro, ritenuto, ralentando - gradually slower

rubato - with unstable tempo, restlessly

ARTICULATION

Articulation refers to how we perform individual notes and sequences of notes, whether by connecting them or playing them separately. It is indicated in musical notation through specific articulation markings.

Articulation Markings

accent - emphasis in a note
staccato - a short, sharp tone
portamento - gliding smoothly and continuously from note to note with a light implication of each new note
legato lift - a staccato note at the end of a legato marking ends quickly with a lift
détaché - long, separated tones
tenuto - hold, sustain tones (full length)
legato - connected tones with no separation

accent  staccato 

portamento  legato lift 

tenuto   legato 

Articulation

E Link the articulations with their correct names.

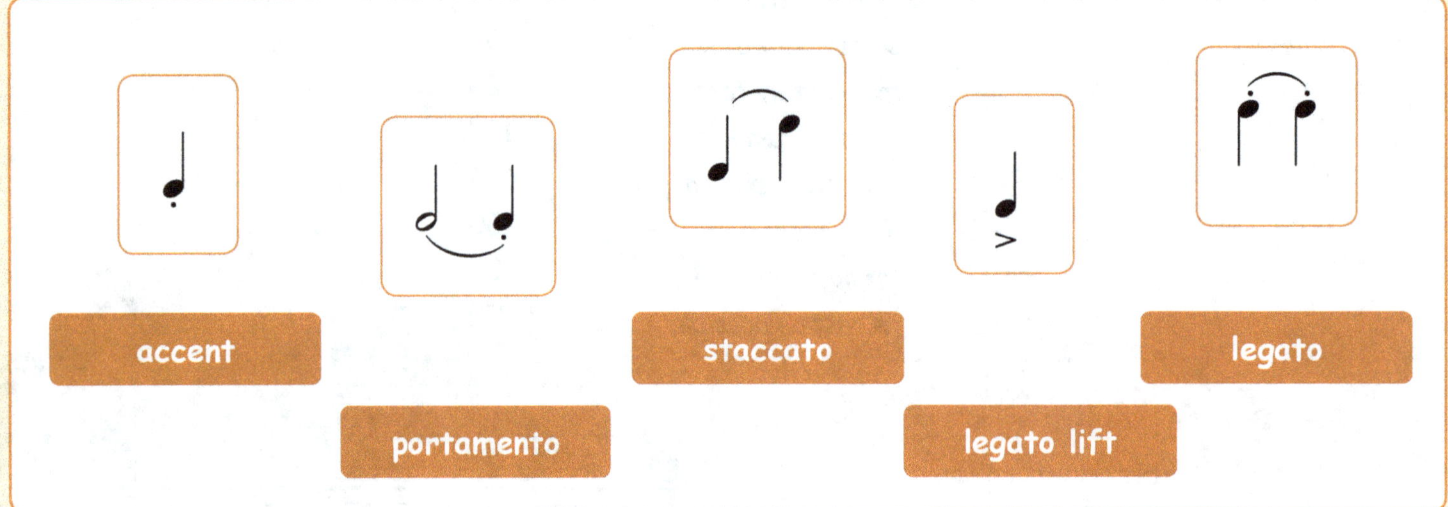

Musical Expression

E Write down the meaning of the assigned articulations.

dolce – ________________   marcato – ________________   scherzando – ________________

MUSICAL EXPRESSION, PERFORMANCE TECHNIQUES

MUSICAL EXPRESSION

In music, **expression** refers to the performance style that blends both rational and emotional perspectives of the performer. It is closely tied to the content of the piece being performed. Expression markings serve as valuable tools for composers, guiding performers to convey specific moods, feelings, or nuances that their interpretations should reflect.

Expression and Performance Markings

cantabile *(kaan-TAA-bee-lay)* - singing	
dolce *(DOWL-chay)* - sweet	espressivo *(eh-spruh-SEE-vow)* - expressively
leggiero *(lej-AIR-oh)* - lightly, playfully	risoluto *(ri-za-LOO-toh)* - decisively
grazioso *(grah-tsee-OH-soh)* - graciously	marcato *(mar-CA-to)* - with emphasis
semplice *(SEM-pluh-chay)* - simply	appassionato *(ah-pass-yoh-NAH-toh)* - passionately
giocoso *(joh-KOH-soh)* - joyfully	con brio *(KOHN BREE-ow)* - with spark
scherzando *(SKAIRT-sahn-doh)* - energetically, cheerfully	con fuoco *(KOHN FWO-koh)* - with fire, fiery

PERFORMANCE TECHNIQUES

Performance technique is usually influenced by a given instrument or voice. Besides specific terms for wind and bowed string instruments, it also includes terms for performance effects.

vibrato - adding vibrations to a tone by a rapid pitch change
glissando - connecting two tones by gliding
arpeggio - playing the tones of a chord in rapid succession instead of simultaneously
con/senza sordino - playing with/without a mute

Bowed string instruments common terms:

arco - playing with a bow
pizzicato - plucking strings instead of bowing them
spiccato - jumping bow stroke
col legno - playing using bow's stick instead of hair

Performance Techniques Terminology

E Circle terms used only by string players.

DYNAMICS

Dynamics affect the volume of sound produced while performing a musical composition.

Dynamic Markings

ppp	piano pianissimo	as soft as possible
pp	pianissimo	very soft
p	piano	soft
mp	mezzopiano	moderately soft
mf	mezzo forte	moderately loud, strong
f	forte	loud, strong
ff	fortissimo	very loud, strong
fff	forte fortissimo	as loud, strong as possible

Dynamic Markings

cresc. - crescendo - get louder
decresc. - decrescendo - get softer
dim. diminuendo - get softer, diminish

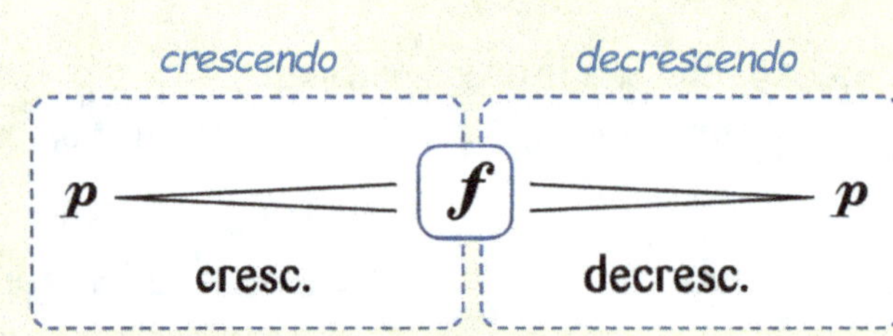

Dynamics

E Line up the following dynamic markings from the loudest to the softest: *ppp, mf, mp, fff, p, f, pp, ff.*

Melodic Ornaments

E Name the ornaments.

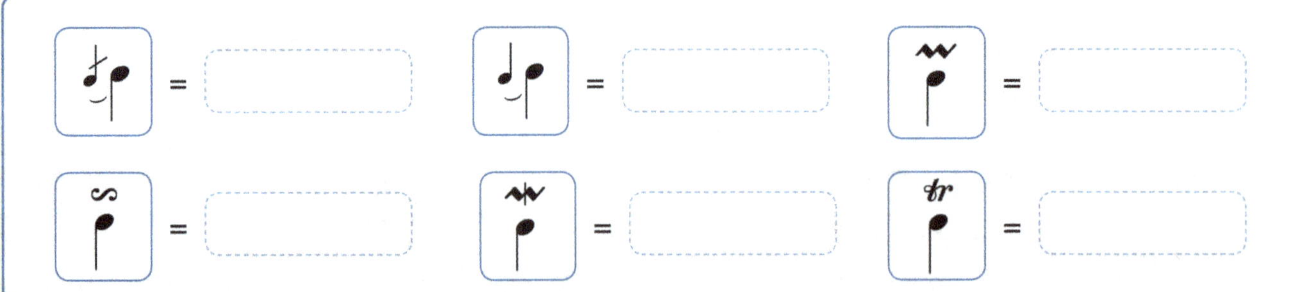

MELODIC ORNAMENTATION

Melodic **ornaments** or **embellishments** enhance and enrich the primary melodic line. While there are general rules for executing common melodic ornaments, significant variations exist among different performers. Playing melodic ornaments can be challenging. The style of ornamentation depends on the historical period and geographical location of its origin, as well as the instrumental skill and preferences of the performer and the notation provided by the composer.

Most Commonly Used Melodic Ornaments (Embelishments)

acciaccatura - (uh-chaa-kuh-TUR-uh) — also known as a "grace note," is a note that is gracefully, lightly, and **quickly added before** the main melodic note

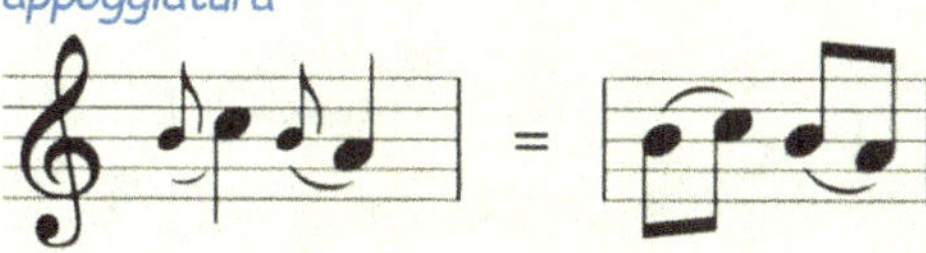

appoggiatura - (uh-paa-juh-TUR-uh) — a long grace note that becomes a part of a melody by **equally sharing the duration** of the ornamented note

run - a group of two or more notes under a slur played similarly to a grace note

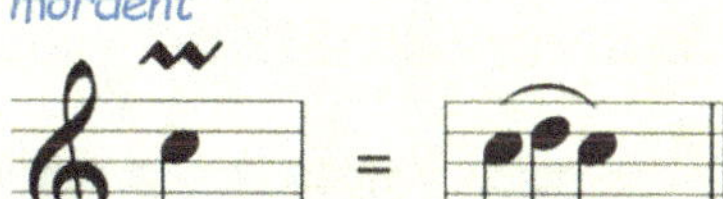

(upper) mordent - a single, **rapid alternation** between a primary **melodic** note and the note **above** it

inverted mordent - a single, **rapid alternation** between a primary **melodic** note and the note **below** it

turn - a single, rapid alternation between a primary **melodic** note, the note **above** it, **and** the note **below** it, creating a **"wrapping"** effect around the primary melodic note

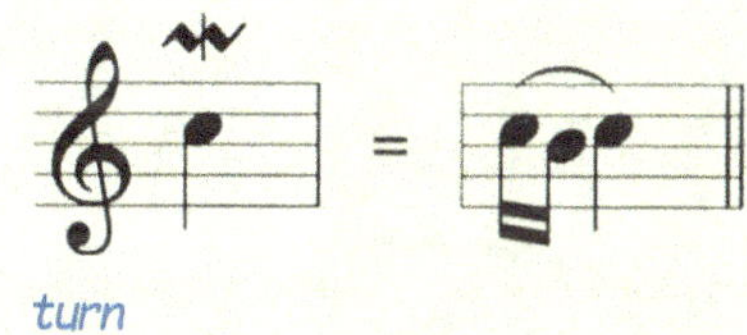

Trill - a rapid alternation between a melodic note and the note directly **above** it. The value of the melodic note determines the **duration** of a trill. Its **speed** varies according to the character and tempo of the composition, as well as **the performer's** skill level. A trill can begin on **either** the embellishing note or the embellished note, depending on the style, historical period, performance practices, and the performer's preference.

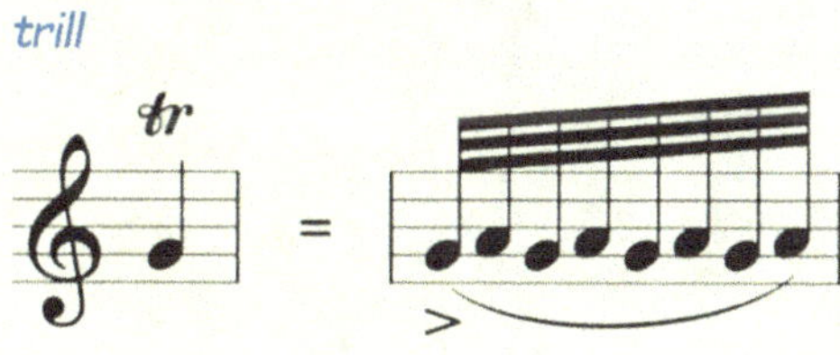

REPETITION SIGNS & MARKINGS

Repetition signs and **markings** are among the most common elements found in musical notation. Their primary purpose is to simplify and abbreviate the notation of a composition.

In the examples below, you will find two versions of the same musical sample. The upper line of the combined staff displays the abbreviated notation using repetition markings, while the lower line presents the complete notation.

Repeating Single Note
The number of small beams crossing the stem (only up to two beams - sixteenth notes) indicates the note values.

Tremolo - Fast Single Note Repetition
Fast repetition without an exact note value.

Repeating Two Alternating Notes
The beams between the notes indicate their values.

Ostinato - Repeating Figure, Phrase, Rhythm or Pattern
Figure - a shortest musical idea or motif used for accompaniment or interludes.

Repeating Section in Composition
Repeat sign - repeating designated section of a composition.

D.C. al Fine - repeating from the **beginning** up to "Fine."

D.S.al Fine - repeating form the **sign** 𝄋 up to "Fine."

Repeating Empty Measures

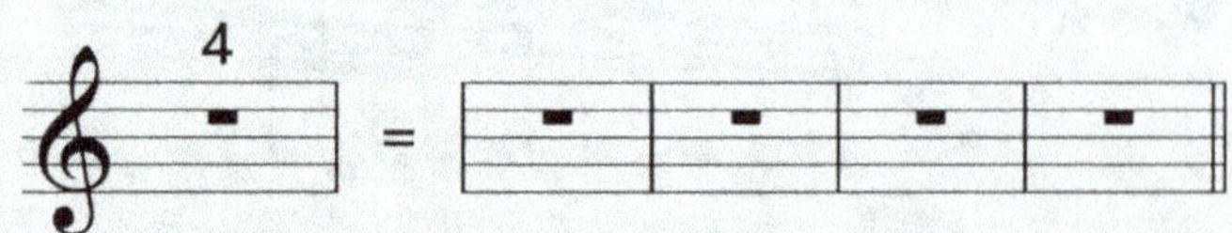

GRAND REVIEW

Rhythm and Tempo. Notation Markings.

Fill in the BPM in the boxes in all exercises. Use the table on page 39.
Try singing or playing the samples using the assigned markings.

E In the opening of Mozart's *Menuet*, Circle all tenuto notes in red, portamento ot notes in green, and lagato notes in blue. Write down the meaning of these musical terms.

tenuto – ______________________________

portamento – ______________________________

tenuto – ______________________________

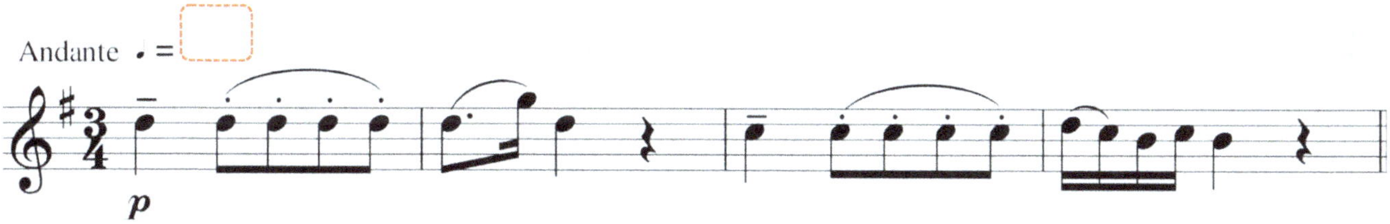

E In Schubert's *Moment Musical*, find melodic ornaments and circle grace notes in blue and runs in green. Then, mark the repeat signs in red. Explain the term "repetition."

repetition – ______________________________

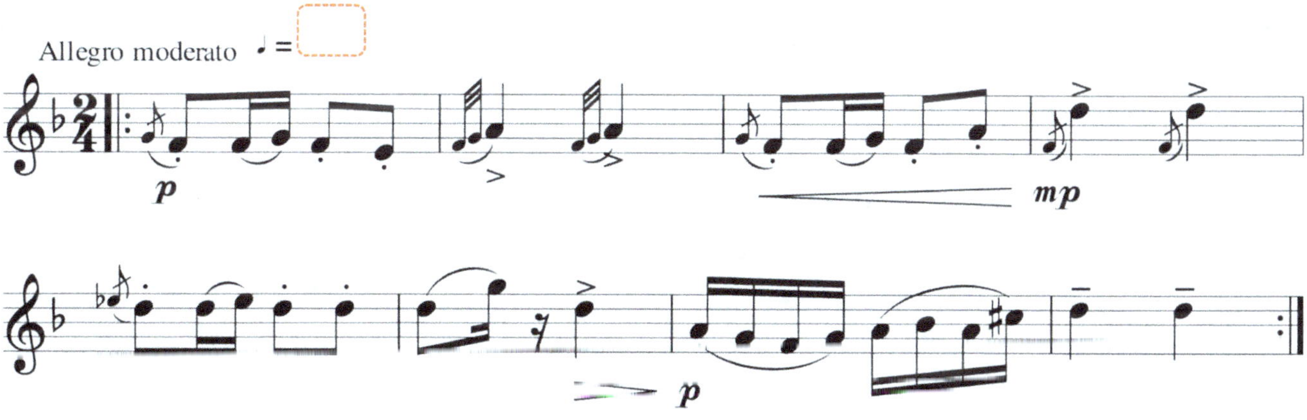

E In the phrase from Verdi's *Triumphal March*, circle a dotted rhythm in red, tied notes in blue, and a triplet in green. Also, explain the terms accent and staccato.

accent – ____________________ **staccato** – ____________________

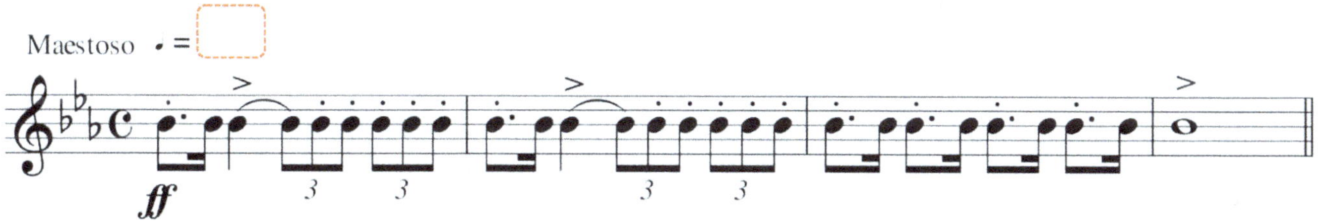

E Following the labels, notate quarter notes and bar lines in treble and bass clefs according to the time signatures. Pay attention to using accidentals within a measure.

E The following notation contains repeat markings.
On the line below, list all the notes you see indicated on the staff.

_ _

Intervals

E Notate the second notes of the melodic intervals indicated by the symbols. Observe the direction of the interval (upward or downward) indicated by the arrows.

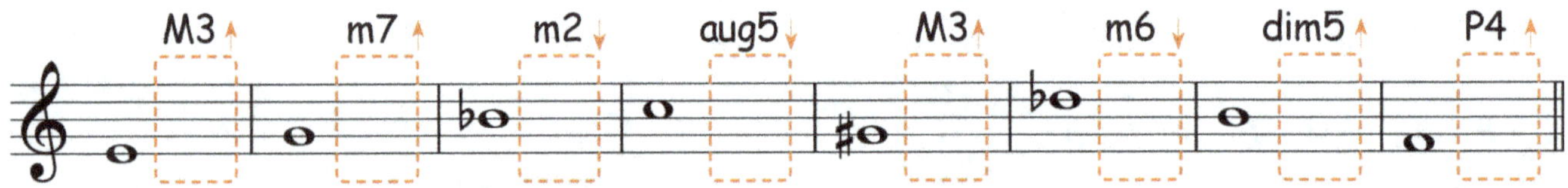

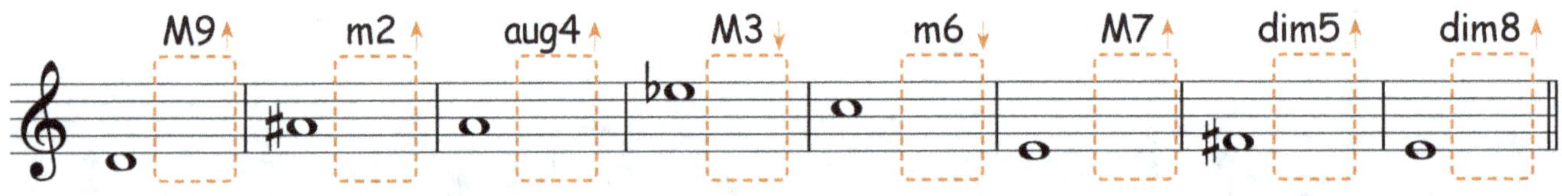

Scales

E From the description, determine a correct scale and write it next to it.

An ancient scale with the m2 as its characteristic interval: _

A scale constructed using only whole steps: _

The twelve-tone scale: _

Possibly the oldest scale used in Asian music: _

A modern scale identical with the Ionian scale: _

E Link thee boxes that belong.

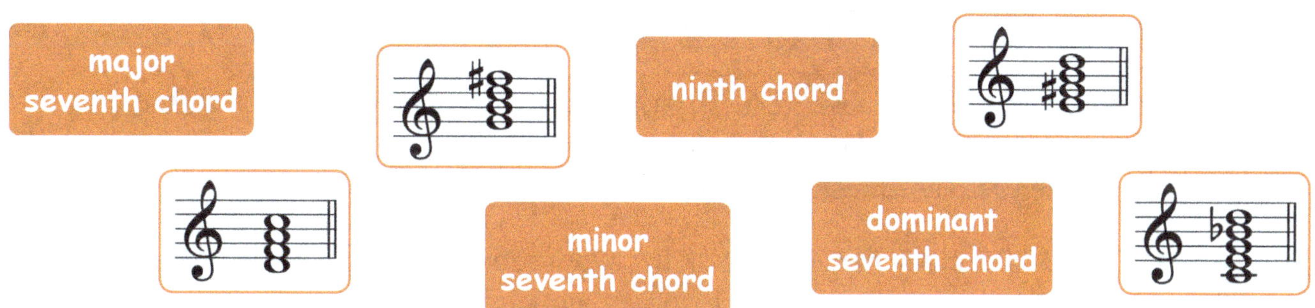

E Notate chords and chord inversions according to the chord labels.

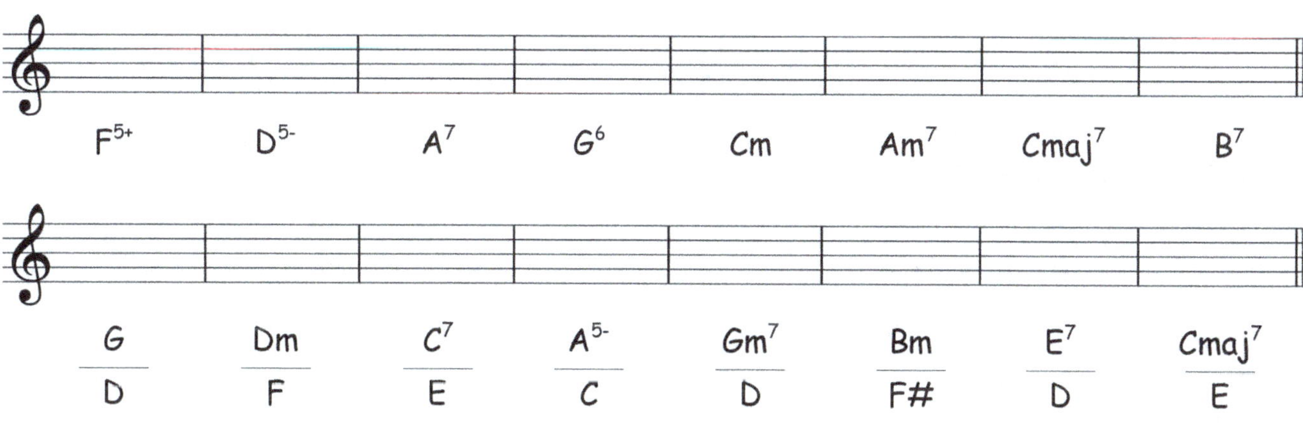

F^{5+} D^{5-} A^{7} G^{6} Cm Am^{7} $Cmaj^{7}$ B^{7}

$\dfrac{G}{D}$ $\dfrac{Dm}{F}$ $\dfrac{C^{7}}{E}$ $\dfrac{A^{5-}}{C}$ $\dfrac{Gm^{7}}{D}$ $\dfrac{Bm}{F\#}$ $\dfrac{E^{7}}{D}$ $\dfrac{Cmaj^{7}}{E}$

Transposition

E In the phrase from Janáček's song "Uncertainty," fill in the chord labels according to their harmonic functions. Transpose the phrase including the chord labels into A and Bb.

PROFESSIONAL MUSIC DISCIPLINES

Musicology is the scientific study of music, focused on research and education within the field. It encompasses a wide range of music-related professions. The most common areas of study include **music theory**, **music history**, **organology**, **ethnomusicology**, and **music acoustics**.

- **Music theory** is a field of study that focuses on the organization, principles, elements, and structure of music. It encompasses various disciplines, including the study of harmony, counterpoint, and musical forms. The survey of musical forms involves analyzing musical compositions to understand their structural characteristics.

- **Music history** explores the rich development of musical traditions. Music historians study the evolution of various musical cultures, the lives and works of composers, and the progress of the performing arts.

- **Organology** is the study of the origins and historical evolution of musical instruments, including their construction and characteristics.

- **Ethnomusicology** is the field of musical study that examines artistic expressions in relation to continental, national, or local traditions. Ethnomusicologists explore folk music, the music of ancient civilizations, and the self-expressive music of various ethnic groups.

- **Acoustics** explores the nature of sound - its creation, perception, and transmission. **Music acousticians** play a vital role by studying the physical properties of musical sounds.

CLEFI'S MUSIC NOTEBOOKS

Clefi's Music Notebooks is a four-part series of workbooks designed to introduce the fundamentals of musical notation and the structure of music. In addition to exploring various types of scales and chords, these workbooks cover the basics of music harmony and chord labeling, helping learners to understand essential elements of music terminology.

CERTIFICATE

OF COMPLETION

This certificate is presented to:

For successfully completing
Clefi's Music Notebook 4

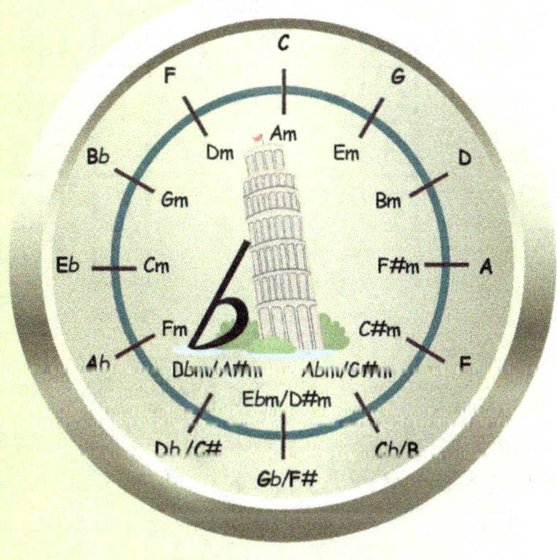

music education teacher

Answer Key to Clefi's Little Crossword Review

Down:
1. A high female voice.
2. A lowered derived interval.
3. The enharmonically exchanged note D flat.
4. A fifth chord built on the fourth degree.
6. The major scale fundamental interval.
8. A fifth chord built on the first degree.
10. dim3.
15. The C major subdominant.
17. The minor scale with one sharp.
19. A C clef (violas).
21. A C clef (cellos).
22. A raised derived interval.

Across:
5. The lowest vocal.
7. A small instrumental ensemble.
9. 9/8 meter.
11. The primary tone row.
12. The first inversion of a fifth chord.
13. A fifth chord built on the fifth degree.
14. The enharmonically exchanged G flat major scale.
16. A complete notation of a musical composition.
18. A measure with just one heavy beat.
20. Two four-tone sections of a diatonic scale.
23. The minor scale fundamental tone.
24. The minor scale with two flats.

Join Clefi's musical family!

Clefi invites you to visit his dedicated webpage and explore the enchanting musical world of Dr. Eva's New Music Education School Series. Learn more about the author and about the content of every volume of the series, dive into engaging materials, find answers to all the exercises, discover more songs, and further deepen your love and understanding of music and music education. Come make music with us!

www.bumblebeenotes.com/clefis-musical-world

www.bumblebeenotes.com/music-publishing